FANTASIES AND IMPROMPTUS

FANTASIES AND IMPROMPTUS

by

JAMES AGATE

Essay Index Reprint Series

BOOKS FOR LIBRARIES PRESS, INC.
FREEPORT, NEW YORK

First Published 1925
Reprinted 1967

LIBRARY OF CONGRESS CATALOG CARD NUMBER:

67-28729

PRINTED IN THE UNITED STATES OF AMERICA

BUT FOR
LEO PAVIA
TO WHOSE UNFAILING ARTISTRY
THIS BOOK IS DEDICATED
I MUST HAVE OFFERED IT
TO THAT
LIONESS OF CRITICISM
REBECCA WEST
FEARFULLY
BY WAY OF DISARMAMENT.

Contents

"Men's principles, notions, and relishes, are so different, that it is hard to find a book which pleases or displeases all men. I acknowledge the age we live in is not the least knowing, and therefore not the most easy to be satisfied. If I have not the good luck to please, yet nobody ought to be offended with me. I plainly tell all my readers, except half-a-dozen, this book was not at first intended for them; and therefore they need not be at the trouble to be of that number."—*Essay on the Human Understanding.* LOCKE.

"Would you say that a flie could drink in this, this is after the fashion of Swisserland, clear off, neat, supernaculum, come, therefore blades to this divine liquor, and celestial juyce, swill it over heartily, and spare not, it is a decoction of Nectar and Ambrosia."—RABELAIS.

Fanfare

Fanfare

"'Little Percy, the hero, was never good at games, but he was always clever. He passes through the usual public school and the usual university and comes to London, where he lives among the artists. He is bowed down with melancholy thought; he carries the whole weight of the universe upon his shoulders. He writes a novel of dazzling brilliance; he dabbles delicately in Amour and disappears, at the end of the book, into the luminous Future.' Dennis blushed scarlet. . . . Luckily, he reflected, only two chapters were written. He would tear them up that very evening."—*Crome Yellow*, ALDOUS HUXLEY.

I HAVE always thought that the most ridiculous of rules which forbids the essayist to throw the word " I " into his reader's teeth. What other would you have a writer put at the head and front of that which he desires to deliver in his proper person. I dislike subterfuge. My hatred of it is as extravagant as my belief that the characters in a book should do as they would desire to be believed. If an author must draw a man of genius let him show us that genius at work, say I. Probably that which induced Mr. Huxley to tear up little Percy's novel was not Mr. Scogan's devastating forecast, but the arduousness of adumbrating that " dazzling brilliance." Were I a novelist—but stop, there is something here which I have to declare.

I *am* a novelist. That is to say, I once wrote a novel, which was published and reviewed. God! How ashamed I was of those extravagant reviews.

Fantasies and Impromptus

" Aldebaran among pasty twinklers," were four out of some fifteen hundred flattering words lavished upon the book by a *Saturday Reviewer* of that day. A day, too, not so very long ago. This was followed by some nonsense which relegated a justifiably popular writer to second place. Horrified, I sent an exculpatory letter to the Great Man, and received in reply a laconic " All praise is good."

I hate false modesty, and will not pretend that my book was bad. It was not. *Responsibility* was, and is, a thundering good book. I spent two years of my life over it, put into it all that I have thought and hoped and dreamed, spun it out of my own bowels and not out of another's. No, silly; I do not mean that the " I " of the story was myself. . .

The reason for the book's failure is no further to seek than the title. *Responsibility* sends a shiver down the back of those abominably-leisured classes. Responsibility, you see, ceases at an income of over three pounds a week. (I will not tinker the blunt phrase which stands for the blunt thing.) The physician of the mistaken diagnosis, the surgeon of the slipping knife go home to dinner with a quiet mind—to them it is no life and death matter. The judge who passes sentence upon the innocent does so with an easy conscience ; for him 'tis no hanging matter. It is right that these things should be. These fellows have done their best, have expended every ounce of energy and skill, unhampered by the fear that, if their best prove not good enough, they must on that night walk the streets.

Not so the labourer, whose predicament is contrary and opposite. The house-decorator who refused to skimp his work would be dismissed at the first conscientious hint. Has not his master accepted the contract on this reckoning, knowing his rival's tender to be based on two actual coats in place of three specified? The journalist who should fail to make his account of a popular murder at least as revolting as the crime would be superseded before morning. Some little time ago, in a corner of South Wales, and within the same month, two men were tried on the charge of poisoning their wives. One, whom I will call Harry Hibbert, was acquitted. The other, Thomas Turner, was hanged. Turner's trial lasting over the week-end, our London Sunday was enlivened with a placard which ran:

TURNER'S ORDEAL
By HARRY HIBBERT
The Hero of Caerphilly.

Now, I have as little doubt that the genius responsible for this monstrosity was duly rewarded as that, failing to come up to the lamentable scratch, he would have been deposed and some viler wretch installed in his stead. All the professions are alike. The musician must starve whose harmony does not fall as expectedly on the public ear as the earnings of the drab into her souteneur's palm.

It is these creatures—house-painter, scoremonger, journalist—who have the sense of responsibility. Woe betide them if by mischance they make the fatal slip into good work. Fashionable surgeon, highly-paid judge, newspaper-proprietor and merchant prince, must, we know, ultimately settle their accounts with God. But that's not yet. My responsible fellow is faced with the more immediate settlements with butcher and baker.

The tale is no new one. In his best novel Maupassant describes the editorial methods of M. Walter of *La Vie Française*. " Puis on s'était procuré, à bas prix, des critiques d'art, de peinture, de musique, de théâtre, un rédacteur criminaliste et un rédacteur hippique, parmi la grande tribu mercenaire des écrivains à tout faire." Of this only two details would be untrue to-day. To-day our racing and our sensation-mongering must be expensively done. Let those babble of Bernhardt who never heard of Rachel, of Russian Opera who can hum no air from Mozart, of Paulo-Post-Impressionism, who never put their nose inside the National Gallery. But let not your racing correspondent mistake a windgall for a spavin. Let not your special reporter omit one sob shaking the delicate frame of the woman in the dock, one twitch of those white-gloved fingers as their owner listens to the evidence of her paramour. *It is these things which sell the paper.* As for your critics of art, painting, music and the play—they shall still be counted among the labourers who are unworthy of their hire.

16

But even if the capitalist—and by this I mean any man possessing more than roof and crust—had not been affrighted at the title, I cannot think that my book would have sold. It is the women who, to the duty of deciding what their lords shall eat, add that of determining the books they shall read and the plays they shall visit. To her butcher's and her baker's books the modern housewife adds her list at Mudie's, and that little account with Keith Prouse. Your elegant dame is for a tale of bawdry prink'd out *à la* Freud, or she has no desire to read.

Responsibility as a title was a mistake. If I had called the book *Skindles—and Kitty* or *Frocked and Unfrocked*, I believe I might have been elegantly thumbed. There is evidence that, in strictly negligible circles, the book was read. I once had the curiosity to ask for it in a circulating library in Lambeth. A copy was produced, and I noted that it had been taken out forty-eight times. It was soiled, torn, dog-eared. Beer and tea, as well as tears, had been spilled over it; there were traces of marmalade, and once I caught a whiff of tarpaulin. It had been annotated. Finally, let me say that my novel is among those which the professional book-hunter has failed to track down. Take that ingenious fellow who, every Sunday, tells us in what novels he has encountered things of like denomination, or those beginning with the same letter—popes and pickpockets, penguins and parachutists. One week he enumerated his discoveries in the matter of prize-fights. Now, tucked away in my ill-fated novel, are four pages to which I gave three weeks of solid work, pages descriptive of a little affair at the Blackfriars Ring —" Darcy's " I called it. Shall I confess that I looked for a reference, how unfavourable soever, to this piece of over-careful writing ? It would have been something to wake up that fine Sunday morning and find myself a concocter of infamous rubbish.

Reader, this is no plaint, but a pæan. What is it to me that the boudoir weeps not when I am bepawed and besmeared and begrimed by the very salt of the earth ? I would not exchange that filthy copy now in my possession for number one of an edition printed on Japanese vellum, royal 8vo, limited to four copies. Granted that I were a novelist whose hero was a man of letters, and granted, too, that I lacked the wit to reproduce the fellow's " dazzling brilliance," I should, I feel, possess the courage of my incapacity and have a shot at it ! My hero should be a provincial come triumphant to town. He should ride the capital as it were a horse. I would show him in the saddle, and make him stand in his stirrups and wave a sword. In my first chapter I should present the reader with " an unpublished manuscript in my hero's second manner," according to it that light of day without which the diamond itself is a dull thing. I should pass over his first manner, which I would have suppose to have worked itself out in the *Scènes de la Vie Mancunienne.*

I would defy reader and reviewer alike. No

description of my hero's features—what concern
is it of mine whether the fellow be tall or short,
fair-haired or myopic ? It is moral astigmatism
which counts. There would be precious few
" tender hints," and no step-ladders of dialogue.
Possibly I might make a compromise in the way
of typographical symbols. Thus :

 a would represent " he said,"

b	» »	" she returned,"
c	» »	" knocking the ash off his cigar,"
d	» »	" advancing to the window,"
e	» »	" and drumming upon it with his fingers,"
f	» »	" with ill-concealed emotion,"
g	» »	" without pausing for reply,"
h	» »	" demurely,"
k	» »	" yet steadfastly returning his gaze,"

       etc., etc.

" The Novel," says your up-to-date reviewer,
" is the most elastic of art forms." And promptly
pounces upon whoso makes trial of that elasticity!
Whereas the great in this line, scorning finical
inquiry into their art-form, pulled it this way and
tugged it that to make it cover such matter as
pleased them. Fielding—I may as well cite a
giant—let down a dedication before his book,
wherein he made those humbugging professions
without which an author of his day had found his
ears in the pillory, his feet in the stocks, and his

middle parts at vulturine disposal. "Besides displaying that beauty of Virtue," snuffles our Henry, "which may attract the admiration of mankind, I have attempted to engage a stronger motive to human action in her favour, by convincing men that their true interest directs them to a pursuit of her. For this purpose I have shown, that no acquisitions of guilt can compensate the loss of that solid inward comfort of mind, which is the sure companion of innocence and virtue ; nor can in the least balance the evil of that horror and anxiety, which, in their room, guilt introduces into our bosoms. And, again, that as these acquisitions are in themselves generally worthless, so are the means to attain them not only base and infamous, but at best uncertain and always full of danger."

Stuff and nonsense! as Betsey Trotwood would have said. Let me benefit by the age and speak to the truth of the matter. Let me affirm that the interest of men directs them to wear the air of virtuous pursuit whilst enjoining upon them to proceed warily lest that pursuit be successful. Let me affirm that no inward comfort of mind can balance that horror and anxiety which the lack of worldly goods affords. That, as the means to attain these are base and infamous, so their possession is a shield against grosser misfortune.

That the poor alone are happy is an old lay of the rich. "La misère! La dèche! la purée!" sighs envious Crœsus with that quality of wistfulness which the *cocotte* knows when, with Dumas *fils,* she cries: " Ohé, l'amour, l'amour! " Shakespeare began this harping on the joy of poverty with all that rubbish about

> " 'Tis not the balm, the sceptre and the ball,
> The sword, the mace, the crown imperial,
> The intertissued robe of gold and pearl,
> The farced title running 'fore the king,
> The throne he sits on, nor the tide of pomp
> That beats upon the high shore of this world,
> No, not all these, thrice gorgeous ceremony,
> Not all these, laid in bed majestical,
> Can sleep so soundly as the wretched slave,
> Who with a body filled and vacant mind,
> Gets him to rest, cramm'd with distressful
> bread. . ."

But how shall we envisage the wretch who, uncramm'd with the stalest crust, tosses upon his attic pillow ? Sleeps he so soundly ? Yon simpering maid, whose face above her bridal gown presages a *réclame* in to-morrow's *Feudal Times,* knows she less delight between silken sheets than yon poor trull who, gallants appeased, shivers in coarse calico and expectation of her bawd ? Poetry is a vile thing, or perhaps it is the poets who are cozeners, hiding the dishonest thought beneath the false glamour of their verse. In poetry it would seem that all is gold that glitters.

After the big liars come the little. Shakespeare descants upon insomnia, these upon disease. The weakling errand-boy, in feverish sweat upon his tricycle, shall console himself with the impotence and cancer of the millionaire in his six-cylindered Sardanapalus. Does a sudden fit of coughing cut short that cheerful whistle? Defies he to no purpose the arrows of the rain piercing the thin armour of a threadbare suit? Shall the boy fall into a consumption? Shall he be a breeder of phthisis? Better, says your well-nourished philosopher, a flowering shrub than a stricken tree. Alas, that this cheating fellow is talking pure bunkum! Alas, that the impotence of the peerage had not yet been established! Alas, that the day is not yet when admission to the Second Chamber is by tariff only, purchasable at auctions coincident with the Newmarket bloodstock sales or the Fat Stock Show at Smithfield! Then for nobility might we read at least the horse-sense of the man of business.

Our Henry used, besides his dedication, a bill of fare showing " what kind of history this is ; what it is like, and what it is not like." Were I a novelist I would show that it is better to be born plasterer than artist ; that a guttersnipe heroine may use her lack of talent to climb the dizziest heights of fame. Brain-considered, the truth about this world is as clay dropped on the coffin-lid of hope. Our job as artist is to mould that clay to beauty. Not moral? I see no immorality in looking truth in her ugly face and transfiguring those lineaments to beauty.

" Partiality is immorality," says Stevenson, " for any book is wrong that gives a misleading picture of the world and life." And again, "I am not afraid of the truth, if any one could tell it me, but I am afraid of parts of it impertinently uttered." Were I a novelist I would write my novels on my knees, revealing as much of the truth about life as life has revealed to me. And that truth, stated in its simplest form, would be that, in this world, it is the second-rate which succeeds to-day. The old, absolute criteria are departed ; the mediocre is level with the good. The odds is gone, and there is nothing left remarkable save that which pays. " A newspaper which is not a commercial success," proclaims your illiterate proprietor, " has not got the breath of life in it. Something is wrong in its very structure : it has ceased to respond to the popular voice. . . . We want a successful news-paper which will preserve the standard of national taste. . . ." Jupiter, then, shall thunder no longer in his own voice. He is to think, not for the people, but with the people. Tonans has abdicated, and the Parrot reigns in his stead. To it, ye Assistant-Parrots! Think with your subscribers! Respond to the popular voice! Lead not, but preserve the national taste if you can! Fill your news-columns with ordure, and your editorials with " uplift "! Lead your soiled public to the well of spoof. Din into servant ears, medium-entranced, that beyond the veil " Cleopatra still cares! " Maunder the sentimentalities of the gallows! Rehearse the ritual of the condemned cell, the menu of the untasted breakfast !

Let us be careful in apportioning the blame here.

Fantasies and Impromptus

It is not Gurth's fault that he likes the tasty stuff. Gurth is just learning to read. Time was when he flocked to the tumbrils. Now, in decent cap and bowler, he awaits the news-cart, annunciatory of the verdict together with the result of the two-thirty. Of course Gurth's taste is low. The point is that low taste is an enormous advance upon no taste. In the old educated days, newspaper proprietors sounded an honourable note; to-day Fleet Street is a-scramble with panderers to vileness. There was a time when the doctrine of *noblesse oblige* held good even among editors. That standard gone, I would make a law whereby every proprietor of a newspaper with a circulation of a hundred thousand should be compelled to run one altruistic other. The staff of this " Daily Utopian " to consist of men who, knowing their jobs, are content to be exact. " Even the reporter has an office," goes on our sentimental Scot, " and with clear eyes and honest language may unveil injustices and point the way to progress. In all narration there is only one way to be clever, and that is to be exact. To be vivid is a secondary quality which must presuppose the first; for vividly to convey a wrong impression is only to make failure conspicuous."

Imagine the grandeur of the scene in which the keeper of the *Utopian's* cage should send for his Parrot-in-Chief.

" Mr. Poll," he would say, " it occurs to me that your story this morning—' Last Moments of the Mincing Lane Murderer '—is more vivid

24

than exact. Kindly have Mr. Parakeet transferred to *The Popular Echo*. Instruct him not to omit any of the more morbid details there, please. By the way, what the hell's the use of telling the readers of that paper what the condemned man *didn't* eat? It's our job to tell 'em what he *did* eat. If the fellow was fool enough to go without breakfast, MacCaw should have nosed what he had for supper the night before."

Yet this I believe and maintain, that in spite of all appearances Gurth's taste is advancing. The decay of the exquisite is not the general death. That which looks like corruption may be the beginning of health. It is not the thresher of progress but the flail of Antique Domination which lays Empires in the dust.

To be frank, it is perhaps as well that I am " not a novelist." There are too many rules. " No psychology! " roars one teacher. " Psychology is for the author, not for the reader. Tear up your analysis of what your hero thinks, and show us what he does! " But suppose that which fascinates me about my characters is precisely that which they don't do? " The work which a writer does all day will more affect his happiness than the quality of his dinner at night? " But how if he have no dinner? Shall he not then take his grand revenge, and write after his heart's and not his belly's need? Shall not he flout Authority if it please him? The Judge has no power to impose deference upon his prisoner who, sentenced to death, is placed beyond earthly subservience for evermore. For him now remain only the fear of God and Mr. James Douglas.

So the artist who, failing to please, withdraws into his own kingdom. There, indeed, he is monarch holding absolute sway. If it please him to be a Socialist he shall be one without let or hindrance. He shall maintain the doctrine and theory of Socialism to be immune from any hurt save the inadmissible one of actual experience. He shall declare that, just as nothing is right about Conservatism except the Conservatives, so nothing is wrong with Socialism except those who practise it. He shall hymn the Communist Creed, yet avow his dislike of bed and board shared in common with yonder noisome wastrel. The Inscrutable, he will demonstrate, has its kinks, among which he will number the insistence that oppressed nations shall invariably be composed of the beastliest individuals. Great poets, he will show, conspire to sing races as treacherous in soul as they are greasy in body. " If an Armenian persists in being an Armenian," said some Teuton philosopher after a peculiarly atrocious massacre, " he knows what to expect." Your starving truth-teller will take this into account. He will realise that, as thunder comes up against the wind, so Reason makes head against Practicability.

The worst novelist has an advantage over the best essayist, as those who frequent book-shops will know. If the book open at a slab of unrelieved print, the prospective buyer puts it down as though it were interleaved with the plague. If her eyes—

26

I have already explained that none but women come to our market—light upon dialogue, then, though the speakers be perfect imbeciles, a sparkle is born and the book sold. The Commandments would not have had half their success if Moses had printed them to " run on." Your novelist fishes for his woman reader by the mere suggestion of emptiness. Men are shyer. For them there is no fly. The best the fisherman can hope for is the conjunction of railway bookstall and fool. The essayist has not even this ultimate device, his circulation being limited to the review-copies sent out by his publisher.

Villiers de l'Isle-Adam begins a story with the apostrophe : " Jeunes gens de France, âmes de penseurs et d'écrivains, maîtres d'un Art futur ... vous avez le légitime espoir qu'il vous sera permis d'y parler (dans la presse) selon ce que vous avez mission de dire, et non d'y ressasser ce que la cohue en démence veut qu'on lui dise— vous pensez, humbles et pauvres, que vos pages de lumière, jetées à l'Humanité, payeront, au moins, le prix de votre pain quotidien et l'huile de vos veilles ? "

The reader has no French ? Je m'en f . . iche! This is a fanfare for my own delectation and none other. The story—perhaps it were better to compound for a quick paraphrase—is a colloquy between a newspaper editor and a would-be contributor. The " jeune plumitif " bases his right to be printed on the score that he is totally devoid of talent. " Je suis, oh! mais sans l'ombre de talent . . . magistrale. . . . Quant à la littérature, je vous le déclare, c'est pour moi lettre close et scellée de sept cachets."

" What ? " cries the editor, trembling with joy, do you mean that you have no literary talent whatever ! "

" I swear to you that such is the case! "

" You boast, sir! " stammered the other, moved in his most secret hope.

" I am," continued the stranger, with a self-satisfied smirk, " a dullard scribbler of the most hackneyed turn of thought, and a peerless banality of style."

" If only it were true ! "

" Sir, I swear . . ."

" Not to me, young man," replied the editor, his eyes filling with tears and countenance suffused with melancholy. Then, gazing sadly upon the young man, he went on,—

" Yes! There speaks Youth! Youth without scepticism, Youth with its illusions and respect for the sacred fire! At a jump Youth claims to have arrived! . . . No talent, you say ? Know then, young man, that to be destitute of talent is to-day to be a very remarkable man, one who has attained at a bound to that to which, formerly, one won through fifty years of struggle, humiliation and wretchedness, to be looked upon even then as a parvenu. Oh Youth! Oh springtime of life! . . Look at me, sir. Look at me and remember that for twenty years I have sought, and sought in vain, for the MAN WITHOUT TALENT! Do you understand? *I have never found that man!*"

The youth produces, unfolds and, inevitably, begins to read his MS. Alas! he has read hardly a word before the editor cuts him short.

"What did I tell you? Your stuff stinks of Letters. You are reading me Literature, and such Literature, too, as would lower my circulation by five thousand in twenty-four hours! Your style alone shows talent! If it were merely witty it would not matter so much. Wit, at a pinch, is saleable. But there is a something about your writing which shows that you are masking your intellect so as not to frighten your readers. And do you suppose that the public likes to be humiliated, to feel that it is being written down to? . . I would as soon print the Directory as print you! That would, at least, serve some purpose. . . The public has an instinct in these matters. It would realise at once that you regard its attitude towards you, whether of praise or blame, as dirt beneath your feet. . . The effort to come down to the level of the public—an effort which obviously only the direst poverty could have forced you to make—is an insult. . . With an air of asking for alms you take off your hat, and with the same gesture fillip the public on the nose—an offence not to be tolerated. Genius may permit itself these familiarities in its books, for then genius shakes its fist in the reader's face with the sovereign intention of raising his head. But in a newspaper these fashions are out of place ; no Board of Directors would tolerate them."

Just as this *soi-disant plumitif* had insufficient nullity for a journalist, so, too, I plead insufficient incapacity for the successful writer of romances. I do not desire that of any book of mine it should be written, " We find in this novel an absence of talent which would do credit to a London magistrate. For its author literature is a book sealed with seven seals ; he is a self-sufficient and intolerable dullard endowed with a triviality of thought and a banality of style, the like of which has not hitherto been known. In short, he has written a best seller." And to him who would write so of these essays I would reply, in the words of an older writer: " Hence Mastiffs, Dogs in a Doublet; get you behind, aloof Villains, out of my Sunshine; Currs to the Devil. Do you jog hither, wagging your Tails, to pant at my Wine, and bepiss my Barrel ? . . . What, are you there yet ? Grr, Grr, Grrrrrr. Avant, Avant ! Will you not be gone ? "

Sarah Bernhardt

Sarah Bernhardt

I

For some whose business it is to write of the theatre it is as though Beauty had veiled her face; so determinate, so utterly beyond repair is the sense of loss. It is not that the stock of loveliness is diminished for a time, as the blossoming earth is subdued by winter : there will be other flowers, but the rose is gone for ever. Those who would charge me here with phrase-making can have known nothing of Bernhardt; she can have meant little to them, and their praise was lip-service. To them such a line as—

> " Elle avait un petit diadème en dentelle d'argent "

brings up no picture the like of which they will not see again; for them *Ruy Blas* can find other Queens, and to spare. Our worlds are different, that is all; those who have not known our ecstasy cannot know our loss. Beauty, in her remainder catalogue, has nothing by which Bernhardt can be measured or imagined.

Even so, I hear it objected that this great actress has been dead, in all that matters, these twenty, thirty years; that she outlived even the memory of her splendours. They would have her dead whose old age and infirmity hurt them so. A

writer in the *Manchester Guardian* shows a finer
temper: " Latterly she had not been able to realise
her heroines for those whose test is realism. Yet
the fragments of her art have been more stimulative
than others' perfections." To know not only
bravery in the maimed presentment but also the
imperishable soul of beauty, to recognise the heart
bound with triple brass, the spirit scorning an end
in sandy deltas—this, the pain of others, was our
privilege. I say without hyperbole that, for those
to whom the art of Sarah Bernhardt was their
most intimate communion with Beauty, her bodily
passing leaves a gap in Nature.

I could never have believed that a Requiem
Mass at Westminster Cathedral could have been
so little impressive. The stage was set at least as
magnificently as Irving's church scenes in *Becket*
and *Much Ado*; the eye was rested by the humility
of brickwork raised to grandeur by its ordering,
offended only by the scalloped edging of the giant
crucifix. The cathedral seemed to wait for some
more imposing celebrant, for Sarah herself, and
then one asked oneself, curiously, what the great
actress had to do with that company of dingy
saints—Simon and Thaddeus, Linus, Clitus,
Clement, Xystus, Cornelius, Cyprian, Lawrence
and Chrysogonus. *Ces gens-là ne sont pas son affaire!*
One had read something of the fortitude of those
last hours. How little of Sarah was conveyed by
that mediæval wail of the " guilty, suppliant, and
groaning! " God's creatures do most honour to
God when they face Death with as high a heart as

they faced Life. This Bernhardt did. If there is a Heaven, then it is not groaning and suppliant that she comes, but as a warrior carving rightful entry like the good man in Bunyan, giving and receiving many wounds.

II

This essay is a critical look round, a note of what our cleverest have said in the past, and stressed recently; a suggestion of where, as an actress, Bernhardt may finally be placed.

In Mr. Desmond MacCarthy's judgment, the best criticism of Sarah Bernhardt, and the finest tribute to her in English, are to be found in Mr. Maurice Baring's *Puppet Show of Memory*. The most perverse, as also the most stupid criticism, emanated from the self-sufficiency of Mr. Shaw. "She was not an author's actress. The only character she gave to the stage was her own." Judging from the whole article I assume that this is meant to be derogatory. In that Shaw is wrong, for to be an author's actress is inevitably to be second-rate. It is only the actor of the domitable personality who changes his mode of being as he would his shift. The fact that Ristori could so alter her features, walk and voice, that it was impossible to believe the Mary Stuart of one night could have been acted by the same woman who played Elizabeth the next, marks her as strictly second-rate. The same applies to Coquelin, whose Cyrano and M. Jourdain were never credibly made

out of the same flesh. Or shall I put it that
the Ristoris and the Coquelins are the first-rate
actors, and that those who put their indomitable
selves upon the stage are, strictly speaking, not
actors at all? Irving was always Irving; upon
that we are all agreed. Bernhardt, says Mr. Shaw,
was always Bernhardt. Agreed again ; that is
her glory. Will Mr. Shaw affirm that Mrs.
Campbell was ever anybody except Mrs. Pat ?
I have the greatest admiration for the genius of
that lady—the only actress on the English stage
possessing something more than talent—and yet
confess that I never saw a pin's weight of difference
between her Paula, Hedda, Magda, Agnes. She
was always the same glorious Stella Patrick
Campbell in circumstances of differing wretchedness. Did she, on this account, fail to be Ibsen's,
Sudermann's, Pinero's actress ? Yes, and the
greater player she. But I do not remember that
Mr. Shaw ever made complaint on this score.
Can it be that " Joey's " passion put out the eyes of
" G. B. S." ? As Mrs. Campbell, so Bernhardt,
and so, too, Duse. No violence to play or author
has ever been too great for the Italian actress, who
would have bestowed her own quality of irony,
resignation and dignity upon a leg of mutton.
When Duse played Marguerite Gautier, a farded
courtesan, she persisted in her refusal to make-up
and insisted upon her own grey hair. As though
Dumas's Armand, Varville, Saint-Gaudens—none
of whom exhibits so much as a *souteneur's* intelligence—would have lost their little of heart and

36

wit to so grave and distinguished a monitress, an Egeria, as Sir Arthur Pinero would put it, a trifle "dusty at the hem." Hear what Lemaître says of Duse's Marguerite.

"Elle en fait dès le début une douce et tendre amoureuse, à qui elle prête l'aspect, comment dire ? ... d'une grisette extrêmement distinguée et un peu préraphaélite, d'une grisette de Botticelli. On ne se la figure pas un instant riant faux dans les soupers, allumant les hommes, s'appliquant à leur manger beaucoup d'argent, ni faisant aucune des choses qui concernent son état. Presque tout de suite, sans combat préalable, sans défiance, sans étonnement de se sentir prise, et prise de cette façon-là, elle donne son cœur à Armand. Elle a même trouvé pour cela un beau geste symbolique, un geste adorable d'oblation religieuse, que Dumas fils n'avait certainement pas prévu. Bref, elle joue les deux premiers actes délicieusement, mais comme elle jouerait Juliette ou Françoise de Rimini : elle est, comme Françoise et comme Juliette, " sans profession "; elle est la Duse amoureuse; et voilà tout.

A " Duse amoureuse " is all for Mr. Shaw's delight. How would he not have inveighed against a Marguerite who was nothing but " Sarah amoureuse "! In the Italian text the story of the courtesan is softened. There is no more question of prostitution. " Ce n'est plus que l'aventure très touchante de deux amants très malheureux, séparés on ne sait plus bien par quoi. . . ." Some members of the Paris audience took this Marguerite

" pour une pensionnaire grondée par un vieux monsieur très imposant." The character, as played by Duse, had nothing to do with Dumas's *cocotte*. Her Adrienne Lecouvreur had as little to do with Scribe's heroine. Both were pure Eleonora Duse. But we do not find Mr. Shaw objecting against this artist that she is not an author's actress.

Bernhardt, Mr. Shaw goes on, " found something in Maeterlinck that jumped with her fancies and made her touch me by her Pelléas as she never touched me in any other part." To put it that way is the very venom of prejudice. As well say that something in d'Annunzio jumped with Duse's fancies so that her Gioconda, etc., etc. No, Mr. Shaw has reached an unripe old age without realising that the great actors are those who count greatness in the number of facets which a single personality can show.

Duse's supreme distinction, says Mr. Arthur Symons, " comes from the kind of melancholy wisdom which remains in her face after the passions have swept over it. Other actresses seem to have heaped up into one great, fictitious moment all the scattered energies of their lives, the passions that have come to nothing, the sensations that have withered before they flowered, the thoughts that have never quite been born. The stage is their life; they live only for those three hours of the night; before and after are the intervals between the acts. But to Duse those three hours are the interval in an intense, consistent, strictly personal life; and, the interval over, she returns to herself, as after an interruption." But great acting is more than an interruption, and that which I have just quoted seems to me only a pretty way of saying that Duse is a greater artist off the stage than on.

Let us thrash out this matter. Duse's greatest moments, Mr. Symons also tells us, are the moments when she does least. He admits that " she does not send a shudder through the whole house, as Sarah Bernhardt does, playing on one's nerves as on a violin." The very expression of emotion with Duse is " the quieting down of a tumult until only the pained reflection of it glimmers out of her eyes, and trembles among the hollows of her cheeks." But should not great acting be more than a melancholy residuum, a banking of fires and hollow, trembling cheeks ? To my mind Bernhardt made it more.

But I must return to Mr. Shaw. " When I first saw Sarah, forty years ago, she had strength and temper enough to make a super-tigress of Doña Sol in *Hernani* for an unforgettable moment in the last act; and although this feat reappeared later on as a mechanical rant introduced *à tort et à travers* to bring down the house once in every play it was very astonishing at first." This is unoriginal nonsense. To rant is to make a noise without suggestion of a reserve of power, and Sarah's apparent reserve was very great. Her *justness* of emotion was equally remarkable; it was the most French of her qualities. She did nothing *à tort et à travers*, and the fact that once in each

39

evening she let off steam simply means that those who wrote her plays took care to provide at least one such opportunity. But to say that she opened the valves without reason is untrue. " She had some natural disadvantages to struggle against; the famous *voix d'or* was produced by intoning like an effeminate Oxford curate; and its monotony was aggravated by an unvarying mask of artificial sweetness, which would have been exasperating in a ballet dancer; yet she forced the public to accept both these faults as qualities." Mr. Shaw will not force me to accept his estimate of Bernhardt as anything except a gap in his sensibility.

The Press as a whole acquitted itself badly in its obituary columns. Alone Mr. Lytton Strachey was exquisite. Mr. Arthur Symons, Mr. Max Beerbohm, Mr. Montague were silent; Mr. William Archer was sober and judicial; Mr. Walkley, if, indeed, it was he who wrote in the *Times* —a matter of which one cannot be sure since that paper's relapse into anonymity — was faintly facetious. Ignoring alike her Marguerite Gautier and her Pelléas, the *Times* memorialist re-hashed a good deal of the old nonsense about coffins, horse-whippings, black-whiskered Brazilians and alligators killed by champagne. Mr. Archer did better; at least he declared his position in the famous Bernhardt-Duse controversy. " Bernhardt's finest period as an actress lay between the years 1875 and 1885. She had then attained full artistic maturity, and had not yet coarsened her talent by the reckless overwork of her European and American tours. During her last years at the Théâtre Français she was certainly an exquisite creature. In such parts as Doña Sol in *Hernani*, the Queen in *Ruy Blas*, Berthe in *La Fille de Roland*, Mrs. Clarkson in *L'Etrangère*, and another Berthe in *Le Sphinx*, her lithe and slender figure and her insinuating, caressing voice produced an unforgettable effect. Her diction was always consummate, and though she lacked the physical resources to carry her to the utmost heights of such a character as Racine's Phèdre, her rendering of most of the scenes, and especially of the opening passages of languorous and hectic despair, was the perfection of purely poetic acting. Here, and in all characters demanding tragic elevation, she was far superior to her great rival Eleonora Duse; but in modern parts the Italian's sincerity and depth of passion produced effects unattainable by the more factitious art of the Frenchwoman. At the same time there can be no doubt that Sarah Bernhardt's range was much wider than Duse's. If Duse carried the palm (as in my judgment she certainly did) in such parts as *La Dame aux Camélias*, *Magda*, and *La Femme de Claude*, she was distinctly inferior to Sarah Bernhardt not only in tragic parts but in those characters of frenzied, nervous excitability, such as Fédora, which Sardou manufactured for world-wide exportation." This is worthy of respect.

And then the contradictions ! Throughout Sarah's career these were never conspicuously lacking. One great critic calls her Hamlet merely

41

lady-like; Mr. Baring says that it was " one of the four greatest achievements of her career "; and that, " with the exception of Forbes Robertson's Hamlet, it was the only intelligible Hamlet of our time." Mr. Baring's criticism is detailed and elaborate, and I quote only one passage here.

" Perhaps the most poignant scene of all, and what is the most poignant scene in the play, if it is well played, was the conversation with Horatio, just before the final duel when Hamlet says: ' If it be not to come, it will be now.' Sarah charged these words with a sense of doom, with the set courage that faces doom, and with the underlying certainty of doom in spite of the courage that is there to meet it. It made one's blood run cold." As, I presume, a merely lady-like performance would not have done.

The *Times* writer, forbearing comment, says simply that Sarah gave us the chance of seeing her as Hamlet himself—" a weak and violent prince, whose character she thought ' perfectly simple.' "

" What is there to add ? " he asks, looking round to see which of her parts he has not mentioned. And remains blind to Pelléas.

It is significant that these full-dress accounts of Sarah give no hint of the quality or qualities which differentiated her from all other actresses. They teem with inessentials; the portraits bring her before us as little as the mere statement of her age gives the sense of time. Perhaps there is no direct method, and we must go to the artist rather than the journalist for some sidelight that shall bring

truth. Some glint of what Sarah was comes to
me in an article written by Mr. Max Beerbohm
in the *Saturday Review* twenty years ago.

" Year by year, when she comes among us, my
wonder and awe are intensified. Seeing her, a
few nights ago, in *La Sorcière*, I was more than
ever moved by the apparition. The great Sarah
—pre-eminently great throughout the past four
decades! My imagination roved back to lose
itself in the golden haze of the Second Empire.
My imagination roved back to reel at the number
of plays that had been written, the number of
players whose stars had risen and set, the number
of theatres that had been built and theatres that
had been demolished, since Sarah's début. The
theatrical history of more than forty years lay
strewn in the train of that bowing and bright-eyed
lady. The applause of innumerable thousands
of men and women, now laid in their graves, was
still echoing around her. And still she was bowing,
bright-eyed, to fresh applause. The time would
come when our noisy hands would be folded and
immobile for ever. But, though we should be
beneath the grass, Sarah would still be behind the
footlights—be bowing, as graciously as ever, to
audiences recruited from the ranks of those who
are now babes unborn. A marvellous woman!
For all the gamut of her experience, she is still
lightly triumphant over time. All this has been
to her, as to Monna Lisa, but as the sound of lyres
and flutes, and lives only in the delicacy with which
it has moulded the changing lineaments, and

43

tinged the hair. Hers is the head upon which all the ends of the world are come, and the eyelids are not at all weary. . . . " Two decades were to pass, and still Sarah was to remain pre-eminently great. And now it is she whose hands are folded and immobile for ever, whose eyelids are closed against the possibility of weariness. For me the genius of this passage lies in the reiterant " bowing and bright-eyed lady." There was that in her acceptance of welcome and tribute which was more exquisite than whole acts of other players.

Just as I find in the carefully moulded periods of this meticulous artist a sense of Sarah's will to conquer not only our hearts but Time itself, so in the phrase of one who is not a professional writer I get the best glimpse of what Sarah looked like. Ellen Terry's " like a cloud, only not so thick "—gives what whole volumes have failed to say. There is something more, which I forget, about azaleas and smoke from a burning piece of twisted paper; the cloud simile is the essential Sarah. To the end she could lean back in her carriage bedizened like Mrs. Skewton, her eyes two burned-out holes of lamp-black in a dead face, and remain the embodiment and parade of loveliness. This was Sarah *quand-même*.

Let me quote a "great moment" by Mr. Desmond MacCarthy. " When Hamlet runs his sword through the arras and, hearing a body fall, thinks he has accidentally killed the king, she stood suddenly tiptoe, like a great black exclamation mark, her sword glittering above her head, and a

44

cry, " C'est le Roi!" rang in our ears, so expressive
of final triumph and relief, that for a tingling
second it seemed the play itself must be over."

Here the quintessential Bernhardt stands before
me, and satisfies the mind's eye.

It is become a commonplace that in physical
resources her immediate predecessor was superior
to Bernhardt. So much has been written about
Rachel's tragic power that I have the uneasy
suspicion that she may not altogether have lacked
the Kemble fudge. Was she, I wonder, something
like our own Siddons, with a dash of Ada Crossley
in *The Messiah?* Yet Rachel is always supposed
to have been the only actress who ever coped successfully with those frenzied sixty lines ending
with the wrenching of the sword from Hippolyte.

> "Voilà mon cœur: c'est là que ta main doit
>   frapper,
> Impatient déjà d'expier son offense,
> Au-devant de ton bras je le sens qui s'avance.
> Frappe, ou si tu le crois indigne de tes coups,
> Si ta haine m'envie un supplice si doux,
> Ou si d'un sang trop vil, ta main serait
>   trempée,
> Au défaut de ton bras prête-moi ton épée ;
> Donne."

The great Clairon frankly confessed that she could
never deliver this passage to her satisfaction. The
difficulty, of course, is to attain the human passion
and preserve the classic grandeur. Rachel may

have achieved this; Sarah threw compromise, and
Racine, and classic grandeur, and the Théâtre
Français overboard, and played the woman as
though she were of our own day. But her frenzy
and feverishness were of the spirit as well as of the
body. And I cannot believe that any actress can
ever have surpassed the pathos of her Phèdre.
Let us grant, however, that Rachel was greater
than Bernhardt in purely classic tragedy. And,
if you like, that Duse outdid her in modern
" sincerity." But there were two " lines " of
Sarah's which, I am persuaded, Rachel could
never have approached, and in which Duse, I am
certain, failed. One was romantic rubbish, the
other pure poetry. Quite how Rachel would have
tackled Sardou and his kind we cannot know;
it is improbable that she could have given us the
tender banter of the church scene in *La Tosca*.
In *Fédora* Duse found nothing that she could act;
in the rôle of Cleopatra she peak'd and pined. I
saw her in *Adrienne Lecouvreur* and, as I have
said elsewhere, in that one performance Sarah
took full revenge. Duse is a greater artist than
she is actress; her talent must be deemed less than
supreme in that it needs masterpieces to feed on.
She is not one of those great players who, in
Stendhal's phrase, " donnent un sens charmant à
ce qui n'en a pas." Duse has not the power to
recreate at the bidding of Sardou's fustian the spirit
of the Middle Ages and the Renaissance, in the
delineation of pasteboard heroics to bring before
us Byzantium and Rome. Half the function of

the great player is to make bricks without straw. Sarah did this, and the mortar between the layers was of molten gold.

In poetry be sure Bernhardt had no peer. Note how even Mr. Shaw puts his finger on her Pelléas, though, as we have seen, he would meanly minimise the passion for beauty by that nonsense about jumping with her fancies. How, in this part, can Sarah not have been Maeterlinck's actress? I remember one scene in particular—a tower in Golaud's castle, and the roadway beneath. At the window Mélisande is combing her hair and chanting. The words are:

PELLEAS. Holà! Holà! ho!
MELISANDE. Qui est là?
PELLEAS. Moi, moi, et moi! Que fais-tu là à la fenêtre en chantant comme un oiseau qui n'est pas d'ici?

It is not possible that anything lovelier was ever heard than that cry from the wings, " Holà! Holà! ho! " or that happiness can ever again so flood the spirit as it did with that onrushing " Moi, moi, et moi! " The whole performance was in a key of beauty as if not of this earth, of ecstasy like that of a child singing. Mark how all reputable critics proclaim Sarah to have excelled in those parts where verisimilitude was of the least value. To see Pelléas raise that face to Mélisande and bathe and drown in those black tresses, to behold the passion of Jeanne d'Arc burn like a flame swaying

47

Fantasies and Impromptus

in the wind, to gaze upon rapt inviolacy, pity and ruth—this was to know the most shining facet of a supreme artist. To sum up, consider this: that in classic drama Bernhardt ranked next to Rachel, that in modern, realistic plays she was within measurable distance of Duse. In romantic rubbish, which she galvanised into semblance of life by personality alone, she was admittedly unrivalled; in pure poetry she achieved heights which no other actress has even begun to scale. In other words, whatever Rachel and Duse could do Sarah did almost as well; that which she did supremely they could not attempt. There is no question of other rivalry. Take Bernhardt for all in all, it is, in my humble opinion, rank nonsense to pretend that the world has ever looked upon her like.

III

If I were asked to name my most exquisite recollection of Sarah, I think I should choose that moment in *La Dame aux Camélias* when the dying Marguerite, kneeling on the sofa and looking up at Armand, would say, " Tu ne sais pas ? Nichette se marie. Elle épouse Gustave ce matin. Nous la verrons. Cela nous fera du bien d'entrer dans une église, de prier Dieu et d'assister au bonheur des autres." The joy which she used to put into that " Ni-chette se ma-rr-ie! " cut the heart to ribbons. They say that Duse's Marguerite died among her pillows—a wistful little creature blotted

48

in the folds of the huge bed, pathetically withdrawn from the world and into her frail, wan self. It must be confessed that Sarah's choice in parting was more spectacular. Once I saw Marguerite die seated on the sofa, her mouth laid on Armand's and her arms round his neck. You could see nothing save the tangled mop of red hair and the exquisite hands. Marguerite's last words had been " Ah! que je me sens bien! " You might have thought her asleep. And then the handkerchief which she carried fell from her hand. I never saw Sarah die in that exquisite way again.

I remember a performance in London of *La Tosca*. The actress was grown too old to care about jumping into the Tiber, and it was arranged that the platoon of soldiers which had shot Cavaradossi should shoot her too. But on this occasion something went wrong. No soldiers appeared, and the curtain came down upon a Sarah baulked of her agonising. And then from behind the curtain proceeded not, as Mr. Symons has put it, an obscure sensation of peril such as one feels when the lioness leaps into the cage, but a sense of very real danger, and a commotion like that of a hundred forest-bred in conclave. The curtain drew up and Sarah was discovered in a fury the like of which cannot be described, beating her breast, lashing her flanks and roaring with open mouth: " Mais tuez-moi donc! Tuez-moi! Tuez-moi! " And, sheepishly, the platoon appeared, lined up, and killed her.

It was on my eleventh birthday that I first saw
Sarah Bernhardt. I remember how small yet how
important I felt as I jostled the grown-ups in the
pit queue. I remember the exact shape and colour
of the sunset on that hot September evening, how
it changed from blood-red to mauve, and a single
star came out. I remember that the poster on the
theatre wall showed a delicate lady in a dress of
the same mauve posing wistfully against a back-
ground of white camellias and silver stars. I
remember the long wait in the dingy theatre, the
growing tension, the blood which seemed to bubble
in my temples, the fever-heat of expectancy. And
then Sarah came. At once, by her mere aspect,
she opened the door to a world hitherto unknown.
Consider that up till then all that I knew was
Manchester, its mean, bowler-hatted men of
business and their dolman-swathed, grotesquely-
bonneted wives. Here was a creature half sylph,
half rainbow. I believe that I cried " Oh! " and
I know that I waited for her to speak in a state of
overthrow not far removed from anguish. The
applause stopped. La Tosca had begun that long,
teasing colloquy, and I knew that just as my eyes
had never before beheld vision so strangely
troubling, so my ears were drinking in sounds the
like of which I had never heard. It is a little
difficult to disentangle what I thought then from
what I have thought since. I can only say that
when, later, I was to read such lines as

Sarah Bernhardt

"... thy body packed with sweet
Of all the world, that cup of brimming June,
That jar of violet wine set in the air,
That palest rose set in the night of life,"

to listen to the ache in Wagner's *Tristan and
Isolda*, or to marvel before the glory of Shakespeare's
Antony and Cleopatra—I can only say that these
experiences had all been forestalled. Let me admit
that Bernhardt is but one page in the never-ending
book of beauty, yet declare that I have known
none more shining. Her acting on that evening
unveiled for me the ecstasy of the body and the
torture of the mind. My small world had not up
till then held cause for pity like this poor lady. For
days after I was unhappy, not because of Tosca,
but because the play was over, and the world had
become empty.

It was many years later that I came to know
Sarah. She had lived down old legends then.
Emperors, they once said, waited upon her, and
Popes failed of an audience. Her chariot was
horsed by captive kings. She loosed none too
tame cheetahs upon unwelcome visitors... Of
all this I saw nothing. The actress whom I knew
was an old lady of infinite dignity. I used to
watch her give lessons on the stage of her Paris
theatre to pupils who were either artists of
repute or humble students. Those who had no
capacity were dismissed with a gracious smile;
upon such as showed a vestige of talent Sarah
would bestow first a scolding and then an infinity

of pains. To the younger pupils she was a veritable Mother Superior, and often the theatre took on the aspect of a convent. I remember Sarah, on her seventieth birthday, seated over the fire in my mother's drawing-room, telling stories and in manner and spirit as young and fresh and radiant as a girl of twenty. I remember her now as she left, gathering round her that mantle of misty grey and filling the October garden with a sea-bird's splendour. I remember the look of affection which she threw to my mother as the carriage rolled away. I remember how we gazed after it, and that presently, from the window, a bunch of flowers was waved.

That this great figure who has stirred all my life should, in delirium at the end, recite passages from the plays in which I first saw her, moves me as for many years I have not been moved. Even now, as I think of that flower-filled room, still figure and quiet face, of that rosewood coffin and gold mountings, it seems to me more bearable to reflect not upon the pathos of transcendent glory and imperishable fame, but upon my childish wonder and that vision which forty years have not dimmed.

Clouds over the Caspian

Clouds over the Caspian

". . . and made a red ruin of that side of his face."
The Fight, WILLIAM HAZLITT.

AT the Albert Hall Georges Carpentier, the
French boxer, defeated the Australian, George
Cook, by knocking him out in the fourth round.
There was never any reasonable doubt that the
elegant French frigate would come to port in the
end however rough the passage, the four rounds
resembling the acts of a play weathering through
storm to happy ending. Why, you ask, should
we have wished for a French victory? Simply
because, whilst we did not know Cook, we did
know and like the Frenchman. That he had not
" made good " in his recent tragic production,
" Œdipus at Jersey City " lent our attitude of
knowing no dethronement the more of grace.
Then are not he and his manager, Descamps, did
they but know it, our own peculiar metal? Asked
why, in that battle with the American battering-
ram, he did not throw in the towel earlier, the little
trainer had a magnificent " Qu'il mourût! "
Grudgingly we admit that Corneille first happened
upon the phrase: the sentiment is English and
pure Nelson. Why should we not idolise valiance
doubled with Hamlet-like wit? How wish Hyperion
aught but luck? How beteem the fists of Cook
visit that face too roughly?

For the beguilement of the earlier hours there

55

was the crowd familiar to these occasions—all that
London holds of brain and brainlessness, of rank
and fashion. The millionaire in wit suffered
unlettered Croesus patiently; bookies put the
peerage at its ease. Mr. "Bombardier" Wells,
"in faultless evening attire," sprawled with
Balfourian grace. Mr. "Joe" Beckett, in a lounge
suit, did anything but lounge, sitting bolt upright
and chewing the cud of bitter recollection. What
disaster, with such an opponent as Carpentier,
may not two minutes afford? Mr. "Kid" Lewis
hid behind a silk shirt a bosomful of challenges.
Mr. Wilde, rapt as a choir-boy on the wings of
"Angels Ever Bright and Fair," unbent to the
Lord Chancellor. This was your true republic.
One heard instructed comments. "Tu verras,
Georges le descendra avec le 'feinte du gauche,
crochet du droit' qu'il a fait contre Beckétt."
"A sa place je l'uppercutterais." "C'est un
fameux knockouteur. Cook ne tiendra pas deux
rounds!" Idly one watched the minor bouts.
Paul Fritsch, the French amateur, easily put paid,
as the sporting journalist has it, to the account of
Tibby Watson, a rugged little Australian with the
snubbed nose of a death's-head. Another Frenchman, one Marcel Nilles, and our own Guardsman
Penwill followed. Slow-moving colossi, they pitted
their masses of unreflective brawn as they were
rival beeves or, bear-like, pawed and hugged each
other affectionately, without damage. More
amusing to watch was the dictatorship of Mr.
Eugene Corri, bluff, debonair, Edwardian,

inferentially the friend of kings. He refereed
this dull match with infinite suavity and sidelong,
birdlike motions of the head.

And then, at last, they came. First Cook, a figure
to fright the eye of childhood. You would have
declared his mask to be composed deliberately,
after the Chinese manner, to strike terror. His
attitude throughout was that of a bull towards his
tormentor. Then Carpentier, slight, elegant,
homme du monde, wearing a dressing-gown Japanese
as the smile of his beloved protector. When he
turned to his adversary with what you divined to
be an entirely gracious compliment, you saw that
the two belonged to different orders. Cook, the
untamed animal, glowered like Aldebaran, the red
star in the eye of Taurus. Carpentier, shining as
Betelgeuse, Orion's particular jewel, had all the
grace of a Grecian marble. You felt that the
sculptor who should make a statue in his likeness
might with dignity subscribe the old pæan : " I
am beauty! I am shapeliness! At the sight of
mine eyes substance of itself strengthens into
just shapes." An unnecessary fuss to make of a
mere boxer ? But there is no " mere " about
Carpentier.

My purpose at the moment is not to describe
the fight, but to inquire whether this slipping grace
is an integral part of the boxer's melody or an
ineffectual, unnecessary grace-note. It has been
said that in beauty there is no first principle, that
our ideas of beauty are derived through what we
know to be useful. Arms are less thick than legs,

because they have not the weight of the body to support. A being of which the arms were the stouter must, to be beautiful, walk upon its hands. Climate engenders in the Eskimo and the dweller by Victoria Nyanza types of handsomeness repugnant to more temperate idea. Thus it may be that beauty is not an absolute thing, but a human conception, that it lies definitely in the eye of the beholder and nowhere else. It may be that the absolute beauty of the stars consists, not in the picture they make in the sky, but in their not bumping into one another; and that meadows tumbling to a moonlit lake are not essentially lovelier than Lord's cricket ground sloping to a ditch. It may be that the lark, intrinsically, is no more exquisite a creature than the earth-worm. That the worm is a fool in the empyrean is of no account ; an underground lark were equally absurd. All that we know definitely is that both are perfectly suited to their environment. And since man can live without larks, but not without earth-worms, is he then to adjudge the worm to be the more beautiful ? But this, surely, is the red herring of anthropocentric prejudice. The usefulness I have postulated is not that of the creature to man, but its own convenient fulfilment. Better to stick to logic and lay it down that we may only compare in beauty things which belong to the same order of usefulness—worm with worm, lark with lark, boxer with boxer. You can make comparison between Nijinsky's pose and the pose of another dancer, Vardon's pedestalled grace and Taylor's squat determination, Richardson's superb carriage on coming up to the crease and another's cringe, Carpentier's poise and Cook's lumbering motions. Of each you must say that beauty and efficiency go hand in hand.

That's the theory. Will it work? If Grace had been a more elegant batsman, would he have made more runs? If Trumper had made more runs would he have been more exquisite to watch?

Let two boxers be perfectly matched morally, mentally, and physically, and the more graceful, on theory, must prevail. For grace is only another term for liberated energy, the spare battalion which wins the day. In equally matched boxers, therefore, beauty is strength.

But is it?

Personally, I am inclined to think that the whole of my last few pages is nonsense; nonsense neatly put together, perhaps, but still nonsense. Probably you can never get two boxers so perfectly matched that beauty will turn the scale. It is rare that a fight between heavy-weights goes the full distance; one of two things generally happens. Either one of the opponents seizes an opening, collects his strength, strikes, and has the luck to find the exact spot long before he has his man beaten on general grounds; or he so batters and reduces him to impotence that he can administer the *coup de grâce* when and how he likes. The first is a boxing-match, the second is a battle; and it is the battle which I go to see.

Fantasies and Impromptus

Mr. Bohun Lynch says that *The Fight* is, perhaps, one of the best known of Hazlitt's essays. It may be so, but it is one of the most difficult to find. Nearly all the editions of the essayist omit it ; in Dent's " Collected Works " it is hidden away in the twelfth volume, among the " Fugitive Writings." To my mind it is the best piece of work about the ring which was ever achieved, or ever will be achieved. And mark how elaborately non-technical it is! Quotations from Shakespeare, the author of Waverley, Spenser, more Shakespeare, Dryden, somebody who might be Milton, Chaucer (or so I take it), Shakespeare yet again, and even a fourth time Shakespeare, with some others—the whole might be the outpouring of a modern dramatic critic. A lucky simile, since it makes my point that it was the drama of the fight between Neate and Hickman which attracted Hazlitt, and not its finical technics.

I do not know the extent of Hazlitt's practical knowledge of the science; I do know that he was careful to make no display of it in his essay. He realised that he was writing, not for the boxing expert, but for the average man who, we are told, is sensual. The average man I take it, goes to a prize-fight in order that he may gaze upon red ruin, not for the ruin's sake, but for the sake of the grit which is thereby revealed.

" Like two clouds over the Caspian," was Hazlitt's phrase—prigged, of course—for the rushing together of " The Gasman " and Bill Neate, and the whole of the essay is in that pictorial

vein. Hazlitt, I imagine, would have had little
sympathy with my disquisition on the function of
beauty in boxing. Between you and me, reader,
I have not much sympathy with it myself. It
recalls to me a picture which appeared many years
ago in *Punch*. The drawing showed a burly navvy
stretching a huge fist over a ditch whence protruded
a pair of diminutive legs ; the legend beneath was
simply, " Nah then, wot abaht that Joo-Jitsoo ? "

" Nah then, wot abaht "—or the American
equivalent—" that beauty o' yourn ? " Dempsey,
and later, Battling Siki, may have justly asked our
elegant Frenchman. I am persuaded that it was
not beauty, but a greater degree of quickness and
skill which enabled Carpentier to get home a
blow on Cook having the force and momentum
of an off-drive at cricket, and to follow it up with
another, resembling in grace and dexterity one of
Shrewsbury's late cuts. Lewis he beat when that
cunning Jew was unexpectedly wool-gathering.
" Box on! " said the referee, who had been caution-
ing them; and Carpentier, ignoring as was his
right the fact that Lewis's hands were still by his
side, boxed on with immediate effect. The Frenchman's defeats by Dempsey and Siki teach the same
lesson, that generalship is of no avail without the
big battalions, and that brains are useless without
the brawn. In each fight Carpentier delivered
blows to the point with all the strength of which
he was capable, blows which would have disposed
of opponents not possessed of exceptional physique.
Both Dempsey and Siki would appear to possess

exceptional physique, against which beauty is the most ineffectual of battering-rams and the thinnest of bucklers. The blows which the Frenchman dealt the American and the Senegalese were as ineffective as rifle-bullets directed with howsoever skilful an aim against the modern tank.

It may be wondered, perhaps, whether the beauty which is accountable for Bombardier Wells's popularity is not also the reason for his many defeats—or, more strictly, preoccupation with that beauty. In a bout which, at a date later than the fights alluded to above, preceded the finest duel *à outrance* I have had the good fortune to witness, that beauty of boxing disposition and execution was as much in evidence as ever, and as punctually followed by inelegant disgrace.

The contest, one of fifteen three-minute rounds, between our ever-graceful hero and indifferent fighter and Jack Bloomfield, the cruiser-weight champion, was a match for no particular title, a piece of sport arranged, as it were, for the fun of the thing. Wells had the advantage in height and reach, seemed supremely cool and confident, and boxed well within himself. His generalship seemed better than usual, and he made Bloomfield look a second-rate boxer which, indeed, in comparison he is. All went well with the ex-Bombardier until the fifth round when, to his own astonishment and, I think, also to Bloomfield's, certainly to everybody else's, he took a short-arm jolt to the point and went down like a stone. He was " out " for at least thirty seconds. There is a malignancy which

shapes this boxer's ends, polish them how he may.
Wells is the one tragedian left to the English stage.

The " big " fight of the evening followed, the
bout between Joe Beckett, who is " after all," as
somebody rather cruelly expressed it, the titular
British heavyweight champion, and Frank Moran,
of America. I shall not, at this distance of time,
enlarge upon what I wrote immediately after the
fight, but give my notes for what they may be
worth. They are as follows:—

" It was obvious at once that the contest was
not to be of the rapier-like quality of the preceding
one. There was, perhaps, too much at stake for
the fine shades, and they were never attempted.
The first round began quietly enough, the pair
wheeling in slow circles and then coming together
like grotesque and monstrous engines of war.
Moran's greater size made Beckett look almost
frail. Very little defence was attempted on either
side, and indeed it must be recognised that between
heavyweights blows are going to get home. It is
the weight of metal which tells in the end, provided
there is no one fatal salvo. Both men telegraphed
their intentions to each other and to the audience.
Early in the second round Moran started to measure
his man with his left, as a preface to the volume of
force coming over in that imminent discharge of
the right hand. One could see the first dawn of
the idea steal slowly over his face, climb up little
by little. A glimmer of understanding would
appear in a corner of Beckett's eye, and the younger
man would try to forestall rather than ward off the

blow. Towards the end of the second round Beckett appeared to hit a trifle low. Moran dropped and appealed to the referee, who appeared to caution Beckett. The third round saw the American make a terrific rush as though he would end the fight there and then. The round was fought with considerable heat, and went greatly in Moran's favour. The fourth saw a perfect deluge of those fearsome rights, Beckett going down for counts of nine and five. The American should have ended it here, as the Englishman was in a very poor way.

" I am not to pretend that the audience was strong in connoisseurship. Perhaps it did not recognise connoisseurs of the boxing art in the boxers themselves. I beg leave to doubt whether anybody present, except a few academic bruisers, cared anything at all for the finesse of thrust, feint, and parry. All that we saw, or wanted to see, was an exhibition of the will of flesh to conquer other flesh. As for mind conquering mind, that was as might be.

"At the beginning of the fifth round Beckett came up remarkably fresh, and the battle turned into one of sheer endurance. The only boxing was now done by the Englishman, who was obviously weakening his opponent with a rain of steady left hooks and half-arm jabs. Beckett's hand touched nothing which it did not disfigure. Now indeed we saw the kind of duel which moved the old writer to talk of the high and heroic state of man. The blows seemed to come with the deliberation of the slow-action camera, and the two men to move like

giants in sleep. Moran was in a bad way throughout this round, and the fight was obviously Beckett's,
if only he could keep his chin out of the way of
the other's right. Moran came up for the sixth
round in great distress, his right eye closed, and
much weakened by loss of blood. Beckett had
matters entirely his own way in this and at the
beginning of the succeeding and seventh round,
when the referee, finding Moran staggering about
and unable to see his opponent, awarded the fight
to Beckett."

Mr. Bennison, in an admirably written account
in next morning's *Daily Telegraph*, called Moran
a "tragic but immensely brave figure." Let me
quote a sentence or two. "The end came in the
seventh round, when Moran, his deep-lined face
daubed by crimson, both his eyes closed, felt around,
groping blindly for his opponent. There was still
great bigness in his heart, his fighting instincts
sharp and all alive, his legs strong, but he could
not see ; the many thousands were riveted to this
more than 13 stone American, helpless, pleading,
blinded, and we were spellbound. A sadly stained
towel was tossed into the ring; men in Moran's
corner had surrendered on his behalf, and Joe
Beckett was the conqueror."

There is nothing here of bloodless technicalities.

The *Morning Post* said that " As a sheer example
of pugilism it was one of the fiercest fights we have
seen in modern times. The half-arm hitting was
terrific. Beckett was superbly fit, and he never
went so well as he did last night over a very stiff

course. Fortune fluctuated. . . . And so in the seventh round the referee very properly stopped the fight. It was a great triumph for Beckett. Still, it must be added that this fierce contest was not boxing in the strict sense of the word; it was sheer pugilism. A great punishing fight, and, after all, the best bout that Beckett ever fought."

The special correspondent of the *Times* called it a " fight to remember. The referee intervened only after about twenty minutes of the most ruthless and courageous fighting I have ever seen. Moran had staggered Beckett with ' Mary Anns,' and the still more deadly right jolt, time and again. Beckett, in fact, was half dazed most of the time. But Moran's right eye was closed, and blood was pouring over his face, and one could almost imagine the Sayers-Heenan fight as the gallant giant staggered, blind, but full of fight, around the ring. Beckett, for his part, showed at last that he was of the stuff that champions are made of, and he deserved his victory."

But it was really unnecessary for these gentlemen to have written out of their own fountain-pens, or for me to have made notes. For the Beckett-Moran fight was described by Hazlitt exactly one hundred years ago.

" I never saw anything more terrific than his aspect just before he fell. All traces of life, of natural expression, were gone from him. His face was like a human skull, a death's head, spouting blood. The eyes were filled with blood, the nose streamed with blood, the mouth gaped blood. He was not like an actual man, but like a preternatural, spectral appearance, like one of the figures in Dante's *Inferno*. Yet he fought on after this for several rounds, still striking the first desperate blow. . . ."

Written in February, 1822, of the defeat of Hickman by Bill Neate, this is a perfect picture of Moran as the referee tapped him gently on the shoulder and bade him desist.

The Ring and the Tan

The Ring and the Tan

GOOD show-horses, when they die, go to Olympia. Once a year, in light-hearted June, the best people signalise a return to the joy of life by gathering together in this classic arena, where once again they make obeisance to the staunchest friend of man, and avow themselves the slaves of an old passion. To throw a leg over a live thing is a thrill that survives in the breast of every boy. It was a neolithic youth, we may be sure, who first grabbed a mane and vaulted on to the back of one of those " Pleistocene Equidæ " which had come down from the Great Ice Age, through the Epochs of the Mammoth and the Reindeer, to serve as food for Neolithic Man. What healthy youngster could resist larder or pantry with waving mane and tail! Thousands of years later a more inventive youth broke off a branch of a tree and, inserting it between the jaws of his mount, strove to guide him with his hand. And the father, coming suddenly upon his son, bethought him of a rope of grass, first for admonitory purposes and, later, for the better convenience of steerage.

I propose to pass over the Bronze Age and the subsequent 7000 years of recorded history, and come at once to the time when horses were first exhibited for public edification. Originally horse shows sprang from the old fairs, where sires were exhibited for the better propagation of the race.

71

Fantasies and Impromptus

This remains to-day the *raison d'être* for the spring shows of the breed societies. But at Olympia there are no breeding classes; and thither the public flocks for the sheer joy of the finished article.

Racing is too often justified on the dull ground of solicitude for the improvement of the horse. I, who know the last remaining function of the utility Hackney to be that of dragging decaying dowagers and comatose countesses round the Park, weep his passing, and sing his translation to the higher sphere of the Show Horse pure and simple. Neither I nor the beautiful ladies who spread out their smart frocks on the little gold chairs of the boxes at Olympia care a row of pins for the artillery horse or light vanner, whose breed we must suppose to be improved by the riding, driving, and jumping competitions taking place down there, in the arena, among the flowers. I do not believe that Lord Lonsdale, handing the rosette to the blushing owner of the best coster's jenny, cares twopence for the donkey's strain. Or that the East End belle bothers her pretty head about prepotency in the Jack. Hers is the donkey-woman's pride, matching the ecstasy of her more elegant but not more horse-loving sisters. The animals have their ecstacy too, only we call it being " full of themselves." Is it to be supposed that Treasury, Mr. Giles Bishop's noble chestnut, had no inkling at Richmond that he was proclaimed the best lady's hunter and the champion among hunters? Or that when he stepped on to the Olympia tan he had forgotten that glory not a se'nnight old? The park hacks, too, do they not know that they must emerge from their rugs in treasured splendour as from her glove my lady's hand? The leapers, I warrant you, know as much about negotiating the green and white fences, trim as those in a child's box of toys, as ever Mr. Kipling's Kittywinks knew about polo. If you are a practised show-jumper you know that "the stile" demands a well-judged take-off and a certain nippy way with your fore-feet; also, that three bars which slope away from you make the utmost call upon horse-sense, feeling for distance, and the faculty to tuck your hind legs well under you. The teams of the four-in-hands are proud that in their veins runs the best blood of Norfolk flats and Yorkshire moors. The coaches behind them are eloquent of England: yonder greys reel off a page from Fielding; the blue-roans echo Sterne; the bays are Dickens.

And this brings me to the harness horse. At Olympia we can see show-ring history in the making. This brilliant chestnut, who won all the championships in this country three years ago and was sold to Holland, annexed all the blue ribands there, and has come back to win more laurels—Knight Commander is his name. Here, too, is the little mare Charm, who won championship at Richmond three years in succession. Gondolier and Dark Legend—the latter from Camilla Lacey, Fanny Burney's home—are fretting to have yet another go at their former conquerors. Here, again, are those marvels of ponydom, Axholme Venus and

73

Fantasies and Impromptus

Miss Freda, miracles of clockwork precision, less than thirteen and a half hands high.

I have a special interest in Venus, the champion of a hundred rings, since once I was privileged to own her dam, to whose victories in Lancashire my sideboard testifies. Perhaps Miss Freda has a trifle more action, quantitatively considered; in purity of rhythm, in sheer effortlessness, she must yield the palm. For no pony that was ever foaled can match Venus standing, or show that neck slipping into the shoulders like a jewel sliding into its case. Olympia is not a battle-ground for these two, but a lists at a royal joust, a stage set for rival artists, for Pasta and for Malibran. Set, too, for that little brown mare, Park Carnation, the wonder of two continents—what Adelina Patti was to the world of song Park Carnation is to the world of leather. Also for Melbourne Fire, the pony which gave me the most exciting three minutes of my existence. It was at the late William Foster's sale. Mel-Valley's Bauble, a little mare 13½ hands high, had fetched 1150 guineas, and in the excitement and with some three halfpence in my pocket, I made an opening bid of 400 guineas for Melbourne Fire. The pony looked like being knocked down to me, and I realised that I should have to sell my War Savings Certificates and my library, my golf clubs, and my remainder wardrobe, when the late Mr. W. W. Bourne, of Garston Manor, Watford, came to my rescue with the welcome, " And ten guineas more! " There was no further bid.

The Ring and the Tan

What are the points of a harness horse? First let me say that speed has nothing to do with it, nor does it matter how often a horse breaks his trot, provided he settles into his stride from time to time, and so "gives his show." Points in the judge's mind are general conformation and the amount and *quality* of action. A horse in leather must go high all round. In front he must " show the knee," or as nearly as possible hit himself in the mouth, delivering the foot as Tom Richardson used to deliver a cricket ball, well out and forward. The sole must be brought down flush with the ground, and not heel first. Behind, the horse must " go off his hocks," *i.e.* draw the foot well under him and kick imaginary flies off his belly with the force of a piston-rod in the engine of the Great Western, Paddington to Plymouth, non-stop express. The faults to be avoided are " plaiting," or crossing the forelegs like Aunt Mary with her knitting-needles, " dishing," which means bringing the forefeet out and round with a flail-like motion, going " wide-behind," or opening the hocks wide enough to admit of the passage of a beer-barrel. These failings cannot be detected at a side-view, and that is why the judge stands in front of the horse or peers at him from beneath the buggy's wheels. But a horse may have all the merits I have enumerated, and none of the demerits, and yet be beaten by an animal with a virtue or so less, and a fault or so more. Because in addition to these there is *quality of action*, by which we mean majesty, rhythm, balance, poise and pose. A horse which carries itself like a simple squire must yield to one carrying himself like a knight, and he in turn to one bearing himself as he were an emperor.

Of all the show-horses of the world the greatest was one which, alas! I never saw. When people say to me, " Ah, but you should have seen Forest King! " they use the voice with which my father was wont to say, " Ah, but you should have seen Rachel! " and which I, in my turn, shall doubtless use for Bernhardt. Let me give a description of this horse in the words of Mr. Geoffrey Bennett, the greatest living authority on the Hackney, and most polished of writers on the horse.

" But, with all his compelling charm and distinction, it was not Royal Danegelt who made the greatest impression upon me that Wednesday nearly twenty-two years ago—the occasion was the London Hackney Show of 1901—for that afternoon a scene was witnessed probably without parallel in the history of this exhibition. The show occupied four days then, and thus there was time for a daily parade of prize-winners, enabling late visitors to examine the victors of the preceding days. McKinley had defeated no fewer than fifty-one rivals in his class—that for four-year-olds and over, over 15 h. 2 in.—and twelve of them paraded with him in the ring. No sooner had the word been given to trot than all eyes became riveted on a brown horse, eighth in order, and sporting but a highly-commended card. There was a hush at first, and then a perfect torrent of applause broke forth, and followed round and round the crowded hall that horse whose action was surely greater than that of any Hackney before or since. None had eyes to see or hands to clap the champion McKinley, nor the second horse, Rosellan, nor Revival, nor Cornfactor, nor the thousand-guinea Cullingworth. There was none in the entire hall who was not shouting and clapping and stamping with delight at the prodigious performance of the brown. And then the gate opened, and the leaders passed out; but the groom with the brown stallion, ignoring the excited steward, circled the now clear arena again and yet again. Then how the people yelled; and the louder they shouted the higher went the horse, the embodiment of equine energy and courage.

" But though the horse did not tire, at long last the man did, and so was forced to leave the ring. And then behind the Royal Box they stood: the horse white with foam, the man supporting himself by the roller, white with excitement and fatigue, and the two surrounded by a dense crowd seething with admiration for a grand horse grandly shown. Gossip anent the horse and his late owner was rife among the crowd. It was said that he had never settled in his class, and had made no show at all, and that the man who now held him had begged to be allowed to run him on parade; that the excitement of owning so sensational a goer had brought about the death of his breeder, etc., etc.

" When at length I could tear my eyes from the horse, and turn up his number in the catalogue, I

found him to be Forest King 5621, brown, eight
years old, sire His Majesty 2513, dam 664 Forest
Queen by Young Fireaway 1367, exhibitors, Exors.
of the late C. Hutchinson, Sancton Grange, Brough,
R.S.O.; breeder, the late C. Hutchinson, Sancton
Grange, Brough, R.S.O. One person in the hall
alone preserved his head in the general hubbub,
and quietly singling out the principal executor,
demanded the horse's price; and being told four
figures, quickly marshalled him to the secretary's
office and wrote out a cheque there and then for
eight hundred pounds, which was hardly accepted
than there entered Mr. J. B. Joel, keenly anxious
to take the sensation of the day at the full amount.
But his new owner well knew his business.

" Forest King made his début in leather in the
same setting in which he had created his wonderful sensation—the Agricultural Hall—where, in
March, 1903, in the hands of that finished horseman, Mr. Vivian Gooch, he carried off the championship for harness horses at the Hackney Society's
nineteenth annual show. His appearance and
action in harness was superb. He appeared in the
ring six times more during the season of that year,
winning the Royal at Park Royal, and afterwards
at the great shows at Bath, Peterborough, East
Berks and Wembley Park, while it was at Cardiff
in the September that he suffered the solitary
defeat of his career. Here the day was very wet,
and the going extremely heavy, and the judges
sent this elegant quality gelding, whose knee
action was the highest ever seen, round after round

of the large ring with Heathfield Squire, who, physically and constitutionally, was one of the most robust horses ever known in the show world, and whose sail-away, swinging style of going enabled him to plough through the mud like a steam tractor. Forest King was not beaten on points as a show horse; he was simply tired out in what was nothing but an endurance test.

" Ultimately the horse went to America, sold for £2500 to Judge W. H. Moore, in whose hands he was never beaten. At the age of fourteen, and having won all that a horse could win, the grand old son of His Majesty was pensioned off and turned out to end his days in a spacious, shady paddock. But he was always full of spirits, and one day about eighteen months later, in the course of a mad gallop across the field, he hit his head against a tree and fell dead. The Judge erected a fine monument over his grave."

Well, that is a long quotation for which the lover of the horse will not, I think, desire that I should apologise.

" Art in its relations with sport, and sport in its patronage of art." The phrase is nice, and it was wisely chosen as the text of Mr. Walter Shaw Sparrow's " British Sporting Artists." Your fox-hunting squire, " the unspeakable in pursuit of the uneatable," has always been willing enough to hang a picture of a good horse upon his walls; it is your great artist who has been shy of the noble animal. The reason is not far to seek. A

79

painter needs to know little about duchesses to make a tolerable canvas of Her Grace who, after all, is a woman like the rest. But to pull off that other affair he needs must know a horse, which is a mystery of a different order. Single-handed, Frith could manage the crowd in " Derby Day "; but he went to Herring for help with his racehorse.

The first thing your horseman demands is that a portrait should look like a particular animal. The old masters evolved a conventional steed, probably that attention might not be diverted from the rider atop, with the result that, to the horseman such pictures are a bore. Many so-called great artists are, to the expert eye, obvious bunglers. Van Dyck's " Charles " is ruined by his charger's ridiculously small head ; Watts's symbol for " Physical Energy " is that purely apocryphal beast, a mare with a stallion crest, club feet, and a broken back; the mount of the Duke of Cambridge in Whitehall, whoever may have perpetrated it, is the sorriest nag ever jobbed by the hour. It is not your art-critic but your horseman who finds the artist out. George Morland, the horseman will tell you, never painted a " good 'un " in his life, for the simple reason that he had no eye for " blood," or that mysterious thing, " quality." He could not put polish on a coat, and never rose above the underbred farm-horse. Quaintly enough, whereas your art-critic will put up with an indifferent horse, your real expert will insist upon a good picture. You cannot fob your horseman off with a map of the lawn at Ascot, showing the Heir to the Throne stroking the neck of one favourite and patting the hand of another. Nor with a multi-populous canvas of the Derby, the reigning monarch leading in the winner, and his consort in the balcony mopping her eyes for sheer joy. These are not pictures any more than the bumping, boring racehorses which used to advertise a well-known brand of champagne are pictures. The anatomical horse by Rosa Bonheur's brother, a cast of which is in every artist's studio, is not a horse. It is an accurate travesty. A real portrait of a good animal is that entitled " The Third Duke of Portland," painted by George Stubbs in 1767, and now at Welbeck. Stubbs is good, says Joseph Mayer, because his animals have that expression which belongs to their kind, and no other. He " refused to illustrate a human feeling, and never showed an immortal soul in a poodle's eye." We know that grey horse on which sits the indistinguishable duke; we know his courage and his gentleness, his endurance and his gaiety. With his throat cleaned out like a game-cock's, his exquisitely-laid shoulder, level back and firm, decided quarters, tail set right on top, with his four good legs and, we feel sure, perfect manners, he is an ideal horse for a gentleman. Stubbs could paint when he liked, but apparently he did not always like. The plate which shows him under the influence of Gainsborough is an equine abomination to which one would not give rockers and nursery-room.

Mr. Sparrow reopens the old question as to how Flying Childers would have fared against Eclipse.

The achievements of the former, a " stuffy " little horse of not more than 14½ hands high, almost exceed belief. Timed at Newmarket by the Dukes of Devonshire and Rutland, and carrying 9 st. 2 lb., his greatest speed in a second of time was 82½ feet, or nearly a mile a minute. Carrying the same weight he covered four miles in six minutes and forty-eight seconds, which is at the rate of 35½ miles an hour. Eclipse was foaled in 1764, or twenty-three years after the death of Flying Childers. He stood over more ground; but one agrees that there is a certain futility in attempting to compare the runnings of horses belonging to different generations. Our author likens it to an attempt to pit Henry Irving against Garrick. That no sane person would contemplate; comparison with Edmund Kean is, perhaps, another story.

Your true horseman is like the fellow who would interrupt your account of a game of golf with young Lightbown-Newbigging by a demand to know whether you mean the Isle of Thanet or the Hampshire branch of that family. Both kinds of snob have pedigree on the brain, but for different reasons—the social nuisance, because his intelligence is too small to cope with relationships of subtler import; the horsey fellow, because pedigree is a mystery to take up the whole of a man's mind. No horseman hankers after the humanities. Philosophy, economics, politics, art—all have some foundation in reason to be come at by philosophers in conclave. These matters abide

professorial questioning: the horse is free and
kicks up his heels in the face of the " British Ass."

In this matter of breeding it would seem that
that which counts is not what the horse has done
in actual performance so much as what he is by
birth, what his sire and dam were, and theirs before
them. Your stud-farm is the home of snobbery.
" Damn it, we must have blood! " or words to
that effect, said Hamlet's aunt to the simpering
young gentleman with the weak legs. From the
standpoint of the stud-owner this daughter of a
line of blood-drinkers was right. A horse without
blood in him would run as fast? It may be
doubted. There's nothing in a name, perhaps,
but everything in the horse's right to bear it.
That two generations of money will breed a gentleman is a fallacy which may hoodwink your Socialist;
ten generations of oats will not deceive a John
Porter of Kingsclere. " The worst sort," murmured
the wit in the play when told that some pleasant
fellow was one of Nature's gentlemen, and your
stableman agrees. There's something in all this,
laugh at it though we may. Perhaps even young
Lightbown-Newbigging's slice from the tee is
hereditary. Sobering thought !

I remember reading in some text-book that if
you had three bodies of different masses disposed
in space, each independent of any attraction save
that of the other two, the mathematician could tell
exactly where they would meet. Further, that the
attainments of the mathematician are so scanty
that he could not predict with certainty about more

than three objects; a fourth must stump him.
(I did not believe this at the time, preferring to
believe that the book was written by a classical
scholar.) Three obvious factors there are about
any horse: his conformation, stamina, and turn of
speed. With these we might deal successfully if
they were not complicated by that fourth item of
the family, which ruins the equation. All the
great authorities, including Mr. William Allison,
have persisted in telling us that blood will tell,
without informing us what, precisely, that de-
nominator will tell. Take Volodyovski, the 1901
Derby winner, "a really good colt, whose dead
failure at the stud may be stated as a problem to
which no one will ever supply a solution." Not
even the British Association, we may suppose.
What boots it to know all about " Katergy and the
colloid complexes "—which may well come to
take the place of our old friend Shakespeare and
the musical glasses—if we cannot tell what sort of
stock will be got, or what show will be made in a
particular race, by a horse whose breeding, make-
up and previous achievements are there for all the
world to see ? Pull him out of his box and he ought
to be a book open for even the tipster to read.

> " Au grand jour du Seigneur sera-ce un grand
>   refuge
>   D'avoir connu de tout et la cause et l'effet ? "

Agreed, Master Thomas à Kempis, that at the
Last Day the knowledge of cause and effect may

not matter very much. Meanwhile there is our life here when, at the beginning of, and during each racing season, such knowledge would seem to matter a good deal.

That, as a general principle, good horses beget good horses is naturally truer of the thoroughbred than of any other race. Some little time ago I made an examination of the record of winning Hackney stallions, which ended in a remarkable discovery. Analysing the awards at the London Hackney Show from 1886 to 1914, I discovered that the sires which had been proclaimed breed-champions had proved themselves, almost without exception, to be failures at breeding prize-winners in leather, whilst those which had proved brilliantly successful at siring harness horses had not a single breed-championship to show between them. Thus Candidate, Reality, Rufus, Connaught, M.P., Ganymede, Hedon Squire, Rosador, Royal Danegelt, McKinley, Administrator, Diplomatist, Copper King, Kirkburn Toreador, King's Proctor, and Hopwood Viceroy, each of them champion stallion for one year and some for two or three, sired between them no more than 27 harness prize-winners at subsequent London shows. Whereas, of those who were never champions, His Majesty got 14 harness winners, Garton Duke of Connaught 34, Gentleman John 6, Polonius 60, Forest King 6, Mathias 59, Mathias AI 8, a total of 187. Not once was any one of these great getters champion, although shown in some instances on as many as five and seven different occasions. Is it not more than a little remarkable that never since the London Show was started have the judges, universally recognised as the ablest we possess, succeeded in predicting the successful getter of the harness horse ? Possibly they have not so aimed, and certainly the offspring of the proclaimed champions have done fairly well " in hand," that is when led at the end of a string. But to breed Hackneys with that object has always seemed to me as sensible as to propagate racehorses in order that they may be stuffed and exhibited on the drawing-room mantelpiece. Prepotency, that blessed word, seems a more dependable quality in the thoroughbred. Take Rock Sand, who got Tracery, who got The Panther, that " perfect dream of a great horse," whose first lot of foals were the best any living man ever saw. " There's richness for you," as Mr. Squeers would have said, and dependableness, too, apart from the betting question. Mr. Allison says simply about The Panther that he was backed for too much money, and that horses do not win in such circumstances. The prices given for thoroughbreds have long been ridiculous, but one agrees as to the cheapness of a mare like Sceptre which, after some successful preliminary flutters, lost the Lincoln Handicap, won the Two Thousand and the One Thousand Guineas, lost the Derby—to the general shout of *nous sommes trahis*—won the Oaks, was defeated at Goodwood by the moderate Royal Lancer, and carried off the Nassau Stakes the following afternoon in a common canter. One agrees that such a mare was " dirt cheap " at 10,000 guineas.

86

If her alternations between victory and defeat could have been predicted, she would have been cheap at one hundred thousand! It was not, apparently, until late in her career that the necessity was recognised for giving her a gallop to clear her pipes on the morning of a race. But all this, together with such old tales as the alleged poisoning of Orme, is now matter for the chimney-corner. Whenever one or two are gathered together in the club smoking-room after dinner, and you hear some such phrase as, " But surely he was out of an Isonomy mare," or " You mean Haddon Marphil, the big chestnut which Alec Gemmell sold to Philip Smith, by Polonius out of Lady Whinmore, four white socks, went a bit on his heel, Mel Valley's King George beat him at Bakewell in 1911. . ." you know, of a surety, that the talkers are beyond the power of Bridge or Billiards. Garrulous to their heart's content, they are there for the evening, absorbed in that fourth dimension which is " blood."

The Happy Cricketer

The Happy Cricketer

Who is the happy cricketer? Surely he who, when stumps are drawn, thanks heaven for the game, however meagre his own achievements.

It is a fine thing to knock a Rhodes off his length, to spreadeagle the wicket of a Hobbs, to hold fast in the outfield that spinning chunk of happiness coming at you from the blue. It is a fine thing, although of a different order, to wend your luckless way back to the pavilion, to be hit out of the ground, to miss a sitter. To strain heart and soul to achieve that which is, apart from the doing, of no importance whatever—this is a gift which God has granted to us islanders alone.

Our brothers in Australia know it not, nor— to hear the croakers—do all our home-folk appreciate it. To judge from the Press you would have thought our friends the enemy to have robbed us that summer of our national honour and country's fame. All because eleven young men had beaten eleven other young men in a trial the result of which affected public welfare less than the choice of a new beadle.

This point of view is admirably, nay, common-sensically, maintained in two books which I have been reading, *A Cricketer's Book*, by Mr. Neville Cardus, and *A Cricketer's Log*, by G. L. Jessop.

That it is the true point of view—*pace* General Armstrong and his redoubtable warriors—is as plain as the nose on all our faces. Probably the only commonplace in Mr. Cardus's remarkable book—the best, in my opinion, ever written on any game by any single writer, Badminton by that condition rendered *hors concours*—is that the Australians have brought to their cricket every quality save the one which renders the others worth having, the quality of pure joy. Better players of the game than Armstrong's melancholy men never handled bat or ball; they have only to smile and no better cricketers ever trod our fields.

In these pages the past comes to life again. Once more we hold our breath as, with one Yorkshire wicket to fall and four runs to get, Ulyett faces Briggs. The little man from Lancashire sends up that easy toss, the big fellow makes his famous drive, the Old Trafford crowd once again pats Ward on the back *before the ball is in his hands*. For once we have beaten the Tykes! In agony we live again through that July afternoon when, in the Manchester Test Match, Richardson bowled his heart out, and the Australians cheered him more than they did their last victorious pair. As I read I am almost faint with pleasure.

" Australia batted first and scored 412. England —with Grace, Ranji, Stoddart, Abel, Jackson, J. T. Brown, MacLaren, Lilley, and Briggs to look to for runs—were all out for 231, and the Australian captain sent us in again. And once more the English cracks were reduced to littleness—all save Ranji who, in Giffen's term, ' conjured ' an innings of 154 not out, out of the total of 305.

Australia needed 125 for victory—a mere song on the wicket. Old Trafford gave itself up to the doldrums as soon as Iredale and Trott had comfortably made a score or so without loss. Then it was that Richardson's face was seen to be grim—his customary happy smile gone. In Australia's first innings he had bowled 68 overs for seven wickets and 168 runs. Yet he was here again, bowling like a man just born to immortal energy. And four Australian wickets were down for 45 in an hour. If only England had given the Australians a few more runs, the crowd wished out of its heart —if only Richardson could keep up his pace for another hour. But, of course, no man could expect him to bowl in this superhuman fashion for long. . . . Thus did the crowd sigh and regret. But Richardson's spirit *did* go on burning in dazzling flame. The afternoon moved slowly to the sunset —every hour an eternity. And Richardson *did* bowl and bowl and bowl, and his fury diminished not a jot. Other English bowlers faltered, but not Richardson. The fifth Australian wicket fell at 79, the sixth at 95, the seventh at 100. The Australians now wanted 25, with only three wickets in keeping, McKibbin and Jones—two rabbits— amongst them. ' Is it possible ? ' whispered the crowd. ' Can it be ? Can we win . . . after all ? . . .' Why, look at Richardson and see: England must win. This man is going to suffer no frustration. He has bowled for two hours and a half without a pause. He has bowled till Nature has pricked him with protesting pains in every nerve, in every muscle of his great frame. He has bowled till Nature can no longer make him aware that she is abused outrageously, for now he is a man in a trance, the body of him numbed and moving automatically to the only suggestion his consciousness can respond to—'England must win, must win, must win.' . . . With nine runs still to be got by Australia, Kelly gave a chance to Lilley at the wicket, and Lilley let the ball drop to the earth. The heart of Richardson might have burst at this, but it did not. To the end he strove and suffered.

" Australia won by three wickets, and the players ran from the field—all of them save Richardson. He stood at the bowling crease, dazed. *Could* the match have been lost ? his spirit protested. Could it be that the gods had looked on and permitted so much painful striving to go unrewarded ? His body still shook from the violent motion. He stood there like some fine animal baffled at the uselessness of great strength and effort in this world. . . A companion led him to the pavilion. . . . That afternoon Richardson had laboured for three mortal hours without success. In the match he bowled 110 overs and 3 balls, for 13 wickets and 244 runs. He never bowled again in a Test match at Manchester."

That, I submit, is the right way in which to write about a cricket match even if you were not present at it. I remember the game as if it was yesterday. It took place twenty-six years ago, and I had just left school. In the morning we had Ranji's innings; the best, I think, I ever saw played by anybody, if you take both the occasion and the quality of the run-getting into consideration. Jessop's century at the Oval Test Match in 1902 ? do I hear somebody say ? To which my reply is that I am writing about batsmanship and not sheer, immitigable impertinence. In the early afternoon, I think immediately after lunch, the great bowling feat began. Ranji I had watched sideways on, from the shilling stand over the place where you bought pork pies and bottled Bass. I remember an August Bank Holiday match against Yorkshire at which, the day being hot, an enormous publican, in the fullest possible habit, after eating three pies and drinking four bottles of beer fell back dead, or as near as didn't matter. The commotion caused by this incident occasioned me to miss a very fine over from Mold—whose delivery always seemed to me the perfection of fairness—and I remember wishing that publicans would choose somewhere else to die. Once on this stand you were virtually marooned. There was no leaving it for any purpose whatever. If you did, you lost your seat. It is astonishing how mind can be made to triumph over matter. But to go back to the match.

I watched Richardson from behind the stumper. He took a very long run, and would come up to the wicket with a sense of irresistible climax and finality. The delivery of each ball seemed to be the one supreme event towards which the whole of his life up to that point had singly moved. Also, you felt that it was the last ball he ever intended to deliver. And then he would gather himself again, and again roll to that crease like some giant breaker urged by an angry sea. And so throughout the innings those great waves spent themselves remorselessly. Other images come to my mind: that of a bow bent to the full, the ball a hurtling arrow. Or say some splendour of the harness-ring, delivering his forefoot as Tom used to deliver the ball. But I think the simile of the wave is the best. Richardson could fling his off-break like spray at the batsman. On the hardest wicket he could pitch outside the off-stump and take the leg. He could, and he did on this memorable occasion, but, alas! not often enough.

My recollection differs a little from Mr. Cardus's account. There was no question of sunset; the game, if I remember rightly, was over about four o'clock. But Mr. Cardus is right in the main; and he has confessed to me that he watched the game from behind the shelter of his nursery-window bars. He would, I suppose, be about seven years old at the time.

Open his book anywhere and you will find no nasty diagrams explanatory of the function of the big toe in turning movements, of the place of the funny-bone in the off drive. You may discover some sound condemnation of the " two-eyed stance," or the modern mania for hitting against the break. But as likely as not you will happen upon some description of one of England's captains possessing " the front of Jove himself, an eye like Mars to threaten or command, a station like the herald Mercury new-lighted on a heaven-kissing hill."

This, by the way, is not Cardus, but an older sportsman, and first in for Stratford-on-Avon. Reading, you rub your eyes and say, "Yes, I saw MacLaren in that third Test Match at Lord's, and he was like that!" Mr. Cardus exercises the true function of the artist, which is to give uncommon expression to common thought.

Such writing about the game as that contained in this book is rare indeed. Mr. Cardus is stylist as well as cricketer. When, in the recent Gentlemen v. Players match, Hobbs played what was for him a dullish innings, did our author record in the columns of the daily paper which he adorns the simple fact that the Surrey crack sat on the splice? No. "Exquisitely as King Charles bestrides his Whitehall steed, so Hobbs sate, immobile yet spry, potential master of the bowling. With that same royal grace which, in life, became our bronze darling, did this idol of a modern people brandish, between the balls, his willow sceptre."

Mr. Cardus did not use these words, but he will! I make him a present of the *pastiche*.

It was with a pang that I opened the second of my two books.

"Golden lads and girls all must,
As chimney-sweepers, come to dust."

Cricketers, too. Not even lion-hearted Tom Richardson can plug away at Time for ever. Time is a stonewaller to outlast Scotton, Barlow, or Louis Hall. There is proof of it in the shrewd guess which I now make that only the old fogeys have any recollection of that greatest of England's bowlers, or of those three determined batsmen, or of Watson who could get " W. G.'s " wicket whenever he liked, and was feared by the " Old Man " to the end.

Of the present-day crowd which throngs the Oval on these latest Saturday afternoons, which throws up its cap for Hitch and holds its breath for Hobbs, how many remember W. W. Read and K. J. Key, Lohmann, Lockwood, and " The Guv'nor " ?

The photographs chosen to illustrate this book tell a sad tale. They are eight in number. Two are of Grace, the others are of Spofforth, Townsend, Fry, Woods, MacLaren, and " Ranji." All these have passed beyond our cricketing ken. I wonder whether the schoolboy who reads these lines can fill in all the proper initials ? They were familiar to me almost before the alphabet, and I shall remember them as long.

Eheu, fugaces labunter anni! Which, being translated, means no more than that time flies, and that that's the rotten part of it. Some of us, reader, are apt to be a trifle *distrait* when we look on at the cricket of to-day. We see old ghosts run-stealing between the wickets, the shade of a Clem Hill catching the wraith of a Lilley on the boundary in that never-to-be-forgotten Test match at Manchester. In old apprehension we sit out with Tate that dreadful hour in the pavilion, watching the rain, and knowing ourselves to be the last batsman for England with eight runs still to get. The rain ceases, we hit Saunders for four, then hear the awful rattle of the stumps. England has lost, and we are back in 1902.

But not all our memories are sad. There is that magnificent one before which, in one spectator's mind at least, all other cricket recollections pale. I allude to Jessop's innings in the subsequent Test match at the Oval. Let me reconstruct the position.

England, on a sodden wicket, and requiring 263 runs to win, had lost MacLaren, Palairet, Tyldesley, Hayward, and Braund—the very names make my mouth water—for 48. The position was desperate, and after Jessop's heart. In his book he tells us that the previous night at dinner he had taken 10 to 1 that he would make 50, and 20 to 1 that he would make a hundred. *He made* 104 *runs out of* 139 *in an hour and a quarter*, and England won by one wicket. Note that the Selection Committee had played him for his bowling. But, bless me, that is twenty years ago!

Even the littlest boys of to-day must have heard of Jessop—Jessop the Croucher, the unorthodox batsman, tornado, whirlwind and maelstrom, bowler and cover-point, too. His first county match was against Lancashire, and he had the unpleasant experience of going in to save the hat trick against Mold who, very imprudently, sent him a half-volley. And so Jessop registered the first of those fours on which he was to base so extravagant a reputation.

His efforts were never pretty to watch, but neither are those of a kicking mule. Who that saw Jessop score a century against the cream of Yorkshire bowling, and take only forty minutes over the job, or watched him come out of his crease half-way down the wicket to meet Brearley's fastest expresses on the full-pitch—who that saw these marvels cares about finical distinctions in style? Jessop may pretend to hug his chimney-corner—he alludes to himself in 1913 as a bald-headed old gentleman—but we know better. In our hearts he is for ever young. G. L. Jessop was a sportsman through and through, with only one vice, that of gluttony. He went after runs " like a shark after a nigger's leg." Let those who demand a definition of sportsmanship ponder this sentence: " In all the many innings I have fielded out to Warner *none has given me greater pleasure* than this."

I fear me greatly that the old sporting spirit of cricket is dying out.

There is little doubt that the championship is a hindrance to the game which it is supposed to help. Too often it leads to the bag's end of mere diplomacy, or even to the game not being played at all.

When Jay Gould, the American tennis player and amateur champion of the world, visited England a year or two ago, he met the English amateur champion at Manchester. They talked, lunched, and appraised the court, but there was no question even of a friendly knock-up. Neither being in championship training, they were content to glare at each other like china dogs on a mantelpiece!

At the recent big chess tournament Capablanca announced that, in future contests when his championship is not at stake, it is his intention to play with more freedom, regardless of the final result. How much nearer the best interests of the game if he were to refuse to allow even the championship to interfere with " the mood to speculate on the possible results of a violent attack."

Games are not businesses, or, if they are, they ought not to be.

As with tennis and chess, so with cricket. Take some recent instances of the championship canker. Take the Lancashire and Yorkshire match at Old Trafford. Yorkshire, it will be remembered, were set 132 to win. At half-past six they still wanted 24, with one wicket to fall. The extra half-hour was claimed. At two minutes to seven they still wanted five runs, Rhodes facing Parkin. Four balls, including a yorker and a shooter, were desperately stopped. A no-ball left four runs to get and two balls to be delivered.

Did Rhodes bethink him of old Robson, who, for Somerset the week before, in similar circumstances, went out for and got his magnificent six ? No, Rhodes bethought him of the championship and those points in hand on the first innings. He blocked the fifth ball, and scored a single from the last. The umpires drew stumps, and the match was left drawn, to the exasperation of fifteen thousand spectators and two expectant counties.

My complaint is not that Rhodes failed to jump out to Parkin, but that both captains failed to jump at the chance of those three runs or another wicket. Can we imagine schoolboys—who are the true criterion in such matters—being content with such a lame and impotent conclusion?

Lancashire's next match provides yet another example of the absence of the will to win. With magnificent sportsmanship, Tennyson closed the Hampshire innings at 5.35, giving Lancashire 70 minutes in which to score 121 to win. When Hallows faced Kennedy for the last over of the day, Lancashire needed 12 runs. Hallows hit the first ball for six, and the third for two. With two balls to go, he again lashed out, was gloriously stumped, and the game ended in a draw.

The point here is that, in the first 40 of those 70 minutes, Lancashire only scored 51 runs from 96 balls sent down. Then, when Tennyson signalled to the pavilion that he would go on for another half-hour, the Lancashire batsmen set to and scored 66 runs in 30 minutes. But too late!

Surely the thing for the Lancashire captain to have done was to answer Tennyson's sporting challenge straight away—to send in his two natural hitters, Norbury and Shelmerdine, holding the more staid war-horses, Makepeace, Hallows, and Ernest Tyldesley, in reserve.

I do not blame Tennyson for not conceding another second. He could not win. He had set the Lancashire men a problem against time, which they essayed to solve too late.

The truth is that participants in a county championship cannot see the trees for the forest. A cricket match is no longer a game but a pawn in a series of games. Alas! that to the county captain of to-day we must apply the old words—

"He either fears his fate too much,
  Or his deserts are small,
That dares not put it to the touch,
  To gain or lose it all."

Whereas the old glory of cricket was that in the breast of every player beat the heart of the poet, James Graham, Marquis of Montrose.

The Piece of Old Brocade

The Piece of Old Brocade

" No artist was ever assisted in his career by the yoke,
by servitude, by enforced monotony, by overwork, by
economic inferiority."—ARNOLD BENNETT.

THE function of the pot-boiler, says the idealist,
is that it shall boil the pot whereby the artist may
continue to exist and to do those things for which
he was created. But your idealist is a rare fellow
for cant, more of which is talked in artistic and
literary circles than in any other, including those
which profess religion. The great bulk of mankind
has, Heaven be praised, no artistic perception, and
remains frankly decent in the conduct of its affairs
other than amatory, wherein it remains normally
indecent. This is as it should be. Those harum-
scarum fellows, the artists, who might be self-
respecting beadles, or pew-openers, or cleaners
of privies, have no right to demand that bread,
with butter on it, should be put at our expense
into their mouths, which they hold open in wonder
before the created world. If a man will traffic in
beauty he must pay the price, which is starvation.
Amongst the axioms strangely omitted from the
text-books of political economy are two which run:
The demand for good works of art must always
be less than the supply.
The supply of bad works of art can never keep
pace with the demand.
Yet one has a sneaking sympathy with good artists

who, when they pot-boil, are so severely handled by those impercipient folk, the critics. Let Mr. Bambullient Bloggs, the popular novelist who keeps open house, put on for the hundredth time his pot in the steam whereof his critics nose a second grouse-moor in Scotland, a third " little place in the country," yet another Rolls-Royce. Do they then fall on him and tear him limb from limb ? No. They leap to his hand, bepaw his knee, fawn on him like dogs upon a master. Some little time ago it was my privilege to take tea with a celebrity whose last book had gone into seven editions on the day of publication. I opened a copy of the masterpiece which was lying about the room, and found that one page had been printed askew.

" Doesn't that annoy you ? " I asked.

" My dear fellow, do you suppose I've looked at the beastly thing ? So long as it sells . . ."

The following week this artful splodger was lecturing, and praised by the critical Press for lecturing, upon the Compromise between Art and Practicability. But let the conscientious fellow whose last book, achieved at the cost of two years of blood and sweat, has yielded less than type-writing expenses—let the careful artist, bashfully, shrinkingly, offer the public something less than his very best in the hope that they will bite and enable him to continue in that necessary operation. Do the critics let *him* down easily ? No. They thunder and fulminate, and trot out a headline in which Homer or Nestor or Neptune, or whoever it is, Nods. There ought to be some secret sign whereby the artist can convey to the critic that he has not hauled down the flag of the ideal permanently, but for repairs only, and that the practicable little pennant has been run up to keep the coast-guard station open.

Whenever I think of the artist who descends to the occasional, necessary pot-boiler, I am reminded of a passage in one of Rider Haggard's books wherein Sir Henry Curtis, I think it is, explains to a native of Central Africa that before descending from the stars he, Quatermain and Good took care to familiarise themselves with the native's language. " Only, my lord," retorts the ebony fellow, " thou hast learned it very badly." A successful pot-boiler, you see, is not achieved by taking thought, but by possessing a genuine, inherent passion for that which constitutes a pot-boiler, and by letting that passion have its way. It is nonsense to say that Mr. Yeats or Mr. Walter de la Mare could have composed the masterpieces of Ella Wheeler Wilcox, that Mr. Shaw could have compassed *Paddy the Next Best Thing*, that Mr. Norman O'Neill or Mr. Gustave Holst could yet oust Mr. Herman Darewski in popular favour. Those couldn't and these can't, and the pity comes in when artists of their calibre and conscientiousness are forced to try.

Once, in my small way, I tried my hand at a pot-boiler, which I proposed to call *Roof and Crust*. I set myself not the *magnum opus*, the *Winter Street* of fervid, indefatigable mediocrity, but the minor

109

task of copying that anæmic twaddle beloved of dressmakers' assistants, shop-girls, undertakers' wives. You can find the kind of thing I mean in the waiting-rooms of unqualified dentists. The reader shall judge of my attempt for himself. Let me say that never, for one moment, did it look like coming off. For it no area-bell, reiterant, had been left unanswered. It was not that the imbecility was not imbecile enough; the trouble was that it was not authentic. " You've not been in earnest," said my publisher when I tried him with the opening chapters, " You can't do this kind of thing for a lark."

Lucinda Cosgrove and her sister Myrtle descended from their first-class carriage in which, surrounded by bon-bons, bouquets of rare orchids and the latest fiction, they had made the journey from the metropolis. They were to break to their bucolic parent, the Squire of Wargrave, the fateful news that Lord Inverforth, a Scottish Cornet of Horse, of ancient and noble family and a rent roll to break the back of Sisyphus, had cast a favourable eye upon Lucinda. The two young ladies, having descended from the carriage, went out through the booking-hall, at the door of which the station-master, making obeisance, expressed respectful pleasure at the travellers' return and got into the landau and pair awaiting them.

They found the squire in the entrance-hall of the mansion changing his boots after a morning with the pheasants.

" Well, my pretties," said he, as hale and typical an old English gentleman as you shall find in a day's march, " and what have my birds to tell me ? "

Lucinda blushed.

" Nay, sweet," Wargrave went on, " there's no matter for blushing, howsoe'er it becomes thee."

"Lord Inverforth has proposed to Lucinda, papa," blurted out Myrtle who, the reader will have guessed, was frankness itself.

" If Lord Inverforth takes a wife from Wargrave, he takes her from a house where men of the highest lineage have sought their brides for generations," said the squire with dignity, uncocking his rifle and restoring it to its place in the chimney-corner.

Now, what's the matter with that ?

For the rest, Lucinda is in love with the under-gamekeeper, a handsome creature of moleskin and corduroy, with a wave of the hair to dismay Marcelle, wicket-keeper's hands, and the manners of the West End stage. The passion roused in this elegant gipsy's bosom by but one drop of Lucinda's modish perfume—Goty's " Nostalgie "—is matched by the spark raised in our heroine's milk-white contours by the mingled odour of bracken and corduroy. Some pagan god has, for O'Bleary's eyes, scooped the wood-brown bottoms of the stout-pot. The very clumsiness of his touch is pathos to Lucinda. He bruises her as she were a flower, and she likes him all the better for it. For him she rejects her rich *parti*, to the dismay of the squire whose ancestral home, despite the landau and pair so obligingly placed at the disposal of the station-master, is mortgaged up to the eaves. Follows a scene in which Inverforth, Cornet of Horse, after Lucinda has spurned him, goes out into the night to cool his brow. A shot. The under-gamekeeper falls. Suspicion rests on Inverforth. The trial. Cornet of Horse condemned for attempted murder. As the convicted felon leaves the little country court-house, with gyves upon his wrist, he recognises in the crowd an ex-bâtman whose life he saved in the Great Push. " I fired the shot! " cries the bâtman who, it appears, has turned poacher. Release of Inverforth. First Offender's Act for bâtman. Wedding bells. Lucinda and her gamekeeper; Inverforth and— you'll never guess—Myrtle, whom he has really loved all the time.

Now, what's the matter with that ?

Think of the cinema rights! Why should the Griffiths and the Stolls go whoring after foreign goddesses, Theodoras, Queens of Sheba and the like, when they have Lucindas and Myrtles at home ?

I will tell you, reader, what is the matter with it: *it is not sincere.* It could never have succeeded. The successful pot-boiler is not achieved by a bulge in the cheek but by a belch from the heart.

The Piece of Old Brocade

The successful pot-boiler must run to a minimum of one hundred thousand words, and I could not stand prolonged immersion in that slop-pail.

The good novel is not written to the order of the public, but to that of the writer's own fancy, how wayward soever. Wherefore my novel shall be stragglesome. It is only the duffers with no point worth making who stick to it. Diffusiveness and not selection is the proper basis of art ! So shall you see the world in all the sands of the sea-shore, and the limitless heavens in a work of fiction.

If ever again I write a novel it shall be based upon a dream which obsesses me with regularity. It dates back to the time when my mother first took me to London.

Entering a chemist's shop to inquire the price of a magnificent piece of old brocade exhibited in the window, I left my mother sitting on the doorstep.

The melancholy proprietor bowed and said, " Good morning, young gentleman, I am Mr. Herman Vezin." Abashed, I quitted his counter in haste, and stumbled over my mother, who rose and pointed to the street. There I beheld a procession of grooms in Lincoln Green, with cockades in their hats, leading a string of white and dappled palfreys. From wallets slung at their sides they took handfuls of gay-coloured butterflies and launched them in the air.

" That," said my mother composedly, " is the

new way of advertising croquet on the Thames
Embankment ! "

That, too, is the plan of my next novel, if ever
I decide to make another venture. I shall call it
The Piece of Old Brocade. It will be published at
seven guineas net, and will have, I am persuaded,
a small, select circulation.

"Thus to Revisit"

"Thus to Revisit"

MR. DE COURVILLE had, perhaps, not so much a happy as a wistful idea when he invited the stars of the eighties to revisit the glimpses of their beloved variety stage. It was with a certain tremor that I took my seat, a shade of anxiousness, not as to how these old favourites would acquit themselves, but as to how we should receive them. Youth—and the audience at the Palladium is a young one—is a trifle impatient, and apt not to realise that an artist who has once been great retains that greatness for those who have the eyes to behold. I remember taking a youngster to see a great French actress turned seventy-five years of age. The curtain drew up and " Oh, but she's old! " said my critic. After the first act he sighed, " How fine she must have been! " and after the last declared with conviction, " She's the greatest actress living! " At the Palladium, on this evening of reminiscence, a young man in the stall next to mine turned to me at the conclusion of Arthur Roberts's song and asked naïvely, " Was he as good as that when he was young ? " Could any ageing actor desire subtler praise ?

One of the best traits of the Englishman is his loyalty to old favourites. If he does not wear his heart upon his sleeve, it may very well be because that rugged organ is not cut out in the accepted shape. Who would expose to view an object that is polyhedral ? For I take it that that must have many sides which has many corners, and I know that the English heart has an unlimited supply of these—as many, in fact, as there are old friends to be accommodated. In this we are more generous than the French, whose appreciation of an artist, more ecstatic than ours, remains taut until it snaps, but lacks the quality of elasticity.

When, as a small boy, I tried to explain to my mother how utterly beyond compare was Vesta Tilley she would smile and say, " My dear, you should have seen Judic! " Well, Judic tried to " come back " thirty years later, and the Parisians would have none of her. I cannot think but that we, in England, would have gone to meet the old artist half-way, would have covered her quavering notes with applause, and thrown, for old times' sake, a flower before her feet. In short, we should have made a better show.

Well, these old artists were quickly seen to be no *vieux ratés*, as our cruel neighbours put it, no " back-numbers " in our kinder phrase. Before I saw them again I had been, I repeat, just a little afraid that the triumph might be on this side of the curtain, in our memories only. What face should we maintain then who, when nephews have prattled to us of Mr. Billy Merson and Mr. Harry Tate, have freely admitted the excellences of these comedians, but ended on the note of " My boy, you should have seen Arthur Roberts! "

Well, now they saw him, and now they knew why, when we talk of " Arthur " there comes into

our voice not only affection but a shade of that awe
which genius always evokes. For genius really
means the power to create, and when we behold
the work of genius, be it only that of the music-
hall artist, we feel in little that first wonder of
Adam when he awoke to the new-made world.

The artists sat in a semi-circle, with Leo Dryden
as their chairman. Each performer wore a domino
which, when Leo gave the signal, he or she discarded
to step forth in the garb of thirty or forty years ago.
The first to begin was Florrie Robina who, in an
incredibly fetching sun-bonnet, sang:

" Oh, said Aunt Matilda to her Sister Margarine."

Now, I want the reader to pause for a moment, and
putting out of his mind the jazz, which is not so
much a rhythm as an interruption, repeat the title
of Florrie's song aloud. If he does not catch the
lilt the first time, let him continue until he
does.

How admirably, in this song, are the characters
of the sisters contrasted, Matilda's sense and her
flightier sister's sensibility! How perilous to the
frailer Margarine would have been any prolonged
stay in London; how wise, how elderly-sisterly
it was of Matilda to cry " Oh! " and so home again.
Charles Lee followed with some patter set to music
which, even in 1888, could hardly have been called
a song. But the dance which followed was very
much a dance, an affair of splits and the high kick,
at which we were as greatly amazed as Shallow

would have been if his brother Silence had doffed bonnet with a cavalier motion of the toe.

Then came Marguerite Corneille, singing " Hullo, Ma Baby! " with a French accent, which found Arthur irrepressible. " I say, Cornhill," he sang out, " are you any relation to Ludgate Hill ? " Marguerite shrugged her pretty shoulders and reproved him in her own tongue. But whoever daunted Arthur so ? He let loose a flood of verbiage composed of all the slangs—the *argot* of the quay-side at Boulogne, of the guide who waylays you outside the Café de la Paix, of the promenade at the Follies Bergères, of the little tables in the cafés of the Place Blanche. He was with difficulty restored to order. " In what part of France were you born ? " he was asked, to smooth matters. " Glasgow! " replied that hero.

Let me recall Sable Fern of the pea-jacket, trousers of white flannel, and " boater " low in the crown, Jake Friedman, Charles Bignell whose " What Ho! She Bumps " enlivened a certain last term at school. The first note of sadness was struck by Dryden's " The Miner's Dream of Home." Leo looked as young and, given that little forelock, as Napoleonic as ever, with a little dash maybe of Mr. Farquaharson's Count Cenci in a cheerful moment. The singer was in full and resonant voice. Two lines of his chorus:

" I listened with joy, as I did when a boy,
    To the sound of the old village bells "

went home to every heart. The phrase is out of

fashion, but I can find nothing better. And now Tom Costello and Arthur indulged in a few " words," Tom accusing his old crony of having been over a few hurdles in his time. Modestly Arthur deprecated this, admitting at most to having been " pretty good on the flat." Then Tom, with his finely featured face, tragic like Irving's, quaintly pathetic like Gerald du Maurier's, once more told us in song about going down with his ship.

It is recorded of Charles Matthews that, at an advanced age, crippled with rheumatism, he would discard stick and crutch and make entrance upon the stage in a flying leap, taking chair and table at a bound. Arthur Roberts achieved something quite as wonderful in the way in which he re-created the illusion of youth. When he doffed his Pierrot's dressing-gown and stood forth the " masher " of the " eighties," it was as though forty winters dropped from him. With his hooked nose and high shoulders, wide sleeves and enormous cuffs masking arms and hands to the semblance of wings, he looked again the obscene fowl of a bygone day. This old man crumpled in his chair became young again, physically and immorally, vigorous in body and in mind, once more the hawk of the impudent promenade. He sang the unblushing days when music-halls were not an alternative form of night-school, with a wealth of expression, a gusto and raffishness which the present-day stage knows not, giving a perfect exposition of a lost art, of a pantomime worth

whole folios of other actors' speech. With Dan
Leno, Vesta Tilley, and poor Marie, he makes the
fourth of the greatest quartet of music-hall performers the world has known. He sang a song
about a lady and a bathing van. *C'est tout dire;*
I, at least, shall not enlarge. In no artist now
before the public can we find such vim, such fire,
such force, so sure a sense of the comic, or such
certain means of execution. Whenever, in my
saunters about the pleasurable world, I encounter
Roberts, I am reminded of Lamb's " Retired
Leisure, to be met with in trim gardens." Perhaps
it is in the vernal and secluded pleasaunce that
we meet least often. Whether on some well-
remembered pavement or in some beloved hostelry
—where genius has a better title to its ease than
idleness can ever own—wherever it be that I meet
this unassuming, methodical old gentleman, I am
ever impelled to make courteous salute. I refrain,
but merely because I would not impose the obliga-
tion of reply.

It shall not be pretended that the eye of these
old artists is as bright, the cheek as round, the step
as firm as once we knew them; nor shall it be said
that these things do not matter. They do matter,
but least to those who see with the eye of memory;
who, ageing in their turn, realise that it is the
spirit and not the body which is the man. When
Charles Lee, doffing his wig, reveals the meek
cranium of eld, even we who are wise in these
matters must refuse to believe that which our
eyes have just seen.

Thomas Hardy has the lament:

> " But Time, to make me grieve,
>   Part steals, lets part abide;
> And shakes this fragile frame at eve
>   With throbbings of noon-tide."

But should not " grieve " be " glad," and is not the lament in reality a pæan ? Glad must these artists be that they are enjoying that fulfilment of living and deep joy of work which exceeds all retirement, idleness, and petering out soever.

A Peg for Balzac

A Peg for Balzac

Sweet Lavender has for me a quality of delight different from that of any other play. You may measure Shakespeare by the pyramids, Ibsen by the mausoleum of Artemesia, Shaw by the Colossus of Rhodes; I place this early Pinero among the seven wee wonders of the world, with the Christmas tree, the old-fashioned, " frosted " card of greeting, the tinselled cracker, the silver paper round the tangerines, Hans Andersen, and Dickens's tale of Scrooge.

There is nothing " clever " about this little comedy, which contains not so much as one foot-pound of intellectual disturbance. But there are times, of which Christmas is one, when we can do without kinetic derangement. The play has been called obvious, sentimental, mawkish. It is all these, but so too are the novels of Dickens. In the theatre on Christmas Eve was a happy audience divisible into two easily distinguishable halves. There were the old fogeys who laughed without waiting for the joke, and were moved less by present distress than by the stirring of old emotion; and there were the young people who fell unsuspecting into the traps laid for them by time-honoured wit, and were genuinely distressed at little Lavvy's woes. To be frank I, personally, did not get quite the old catch at the heart when Dick sits down to write the letter to Clem, or suffer the old degree of agony entailed by the absence of a messenger, or know the rapture of the suddenly recollected Bulger. But there were many in the audience who felt these throes for the first time, and therefore at the greatest of their force.

It is too often suggested that the well-made play is a theatrical crime. It is nothing of the sort. I would respectfully suggest to some of our duller intelligentsia that they should deign to study this little comedy upon which they curiously descant as upon a fine specimen of the embalmer's art. I would ask them to consider the five-fold utility of the humblest of the characters, Bulger the hairdresser. Bulger it is who prepares us for the disreputable Phenyl, the flight of Ruth, and is on hand to deliver the letter. Were it not for Bulger we should not know whether, at the beginning of the third act, Wedderburn is alive or dead, or that the Gilfillians are staying in the house. Then I should ask them to consider the teaspoon, and how the use of it to weight Minnie's letter makes relevant all that admirable talk about washing and wiping. I should point with ecstasy to the " long arm of coincidence," which, it is not generally recognised, may be a good arm as well as a bad. They are good coincidences which secure that Wedderburn's adopted son shall fall in love with Wedderburn's illegitimate daughter, and that Phenyl's uncle should leave Phenyl a fortune invested in Wedderburn's bank, which smashes on the very day that Phenyl hears of his good luck. In truth, these things are not coincidences at all.

128

It is not a coincidence that, in yonder chess-problem, the poor king shall in two moves be mated, whithersoever he turn. Nor is it a coincidence that the cadenza and the coda shall prove an echo. Nor yet that the garland of blue roses tied with pink ribbon shall be found to repeat itself on my wall one hundred and seventy times. These things are the essential design, no more and no less than the coincidences of *Sweet Lavender* are the stuff and texture and pattern of the play. I would have even more of them. I would have Dr. Delaney and Mrs. Gilfillian conceive a mutual passion which, with Wedderburn hinting at " making an honest woman " of Ruth, would balance the stage with four pairs of lovers grouped about Phenyl, forlorn yet not disconsolate, wedded to his bottle as Bunthorne to his lily. I would endow Ruth with two more daughters who should comfort Mr. Bulger, the hairdresser, and Mr. Maw, the solicitor. It is good that once a year these innocent ardours should be allowed the full stage. It is good that, at Christmas, passion should forsake its anæmic, repertory air, and bear some resemblance to the red robins of the frost-bespangled cards. It is to a performance of *Sweet Lavender* that, on Christmas Eve, I would summon the characters of that master. Scrooge would take a box for the Linkinwaters; the Cheerybles escort the Murdstones and dig them in the ribs; Joe Gargery should fling his arms round Mr. Dombey's neck, and bedew that solemn choker with his tears.

Where, asks the reader ruminatively, have I

met that idea before ? I will tell him. If he has been very, very lucky he has met it in Charles de Lovenjoul's *Histoire des Œuvres de Balzac*, published by Calmann Lévy in 1879. Of all the books in my library this is the one I prize most. Others may, and do, possess Cerfberr and Christophe's *Répertoire de la Comédie Humaine*, but I have heard none boast of the Lovenjoul. It is to be imagined that Mr. George Moore and Mr. Edmund Gosse must possess copies; but they, and indeed all our critics, are singularly silent nowadays about the greatest of all novelists. It may be that Balzac, like the Solar System, is taken for granted by the rising generation; but I think it much more likely that he is ignored. The fickle French ceased to read him long ago; that indigestible chronicler, Marcel Proust, and the industrious purveyor of *La Garçonne* being more to their taste to-day.

It is my intention to transcribe part of one of the miraculous chapters of the *Histoire*, a chapter which Lovenjoul lifted whole from Albéric Second's *A quoi tient l'amour*. It is called *La Centième Représentation de Mercadet*. Second relates how he attended the hundredth performance of Balzac's posthumous *Mercadet le Faiseur* at the Theâtre du Gymnase, and how a stranger occupying the seat next to him, whose opera-glasses were engraved with the letters E. and R. surmounted by a coronet, waved his hand to the empty stalls and boxes, and distributed distinguished little bows. Suddenly the stranger turned to Second and spoke, whereupon the following colloquy took place. I give the rest in Second's words:—

" ' My dear fellow-countryman,' said my neighbour, ' for if I mistake not, you too come from Charente, I am delighted to see you.'

" ' To whom have I the honour of speaking ? ' I replied, with a considerable degree of surprise.

" My interlocutor drew from his pocket a card, which he presented with an air of extreme gallantry. In my astonishment I nearly cried out aloud. The card bore the words: Count Eugène de Rastignac.

" ' M. de Rastignac ? ' I asked incredulously.

" ' In person.'

" ' Born at Ruffic ? '

" ' Precisely.'

" ' The cousin of Madame de Beauséant ? '

" ' Himself.'

" ' Who once inhabited the *pension* of Madame Vauquer, *née* de Conflans ? '

" ' Correct.'

" ' And knew Vautrin and the père Goriot ? '

" ' Intimately.'

" ' In fact, you are really alive ? ' I asked.

" M. de Rastignac smiled.

" ' Do I look like a ghost ? ' he said, twirling his moustache.

" Here the Count touched me on the forehead, and at once the stalls and boxes, which had previously been empty, became full.

" ' Now, look,' said M. de Rastignac. ' They are all here,' went on Madame Vauquer's former lodger. ' The principal personages of the Human

131

Comedy have done like you: they have assembled to salute the hundredth performance of *Mercadet*, and to applaud so long and so loud that the noise of their bravos shall stir Balzac in his tomb.'

" ' Nathan! ' he cried.

" ' Count ? '

" ' Where and when your next play ? '

" ' I am just finishing a trifle for the Ambigu-Comique.'

" ' Keep me a box.'

" ' Your name is already inscribed.'

" ' Du Bruel ? '

" ' Present ! '

" ' Permit me to tell you that since your election to the Academy you have become deuced lazy!'

" ' Lazy ? The Vaudeville is rehearsing a five-act play of mine and the Variétés a two-act comedy.'

" ' Good news! Do I see your wife anywhere ? '

" ' Tullia is in the third row of boxes.'

" ' Alone ? '

" ' With La Palférine.'

" ' Tell me, Horace, is it true that the poor Vidame de Pamiers is sinking ? '

" ' He died at five o'clock this afternoon.'

" ' Don't tell me that Bianchon, the famous specialist, has taken to killing his patients like a country leech! '

" ' Mon cher, he died of his ninety-seven years ! '

" Some reflections follow and then:

" ' Is it true that La Palferine " ne voit plus Madame de Rochegude ? ' "

" ' He has renewed his faithfulness to Tullia,

and tells everybody that her husband's cook is the greatest artist in Paris.'

" ' Madame de Rochegude is still alive ? '

" ' She is in a box on the ground-floor.'

" ' Who is with her ? '

" ' Conti.'

" ' The composer ? '

" ' Of course. Don't you know the old song:

> " Et l'on revient toujours
> A ses premiers amours! ' "

" I was anxious to have a glimpse of this artificial blonde whom the young Baron Calyste du Guénic (See *Béatrix*) had so greatly adored, and I prayed M. de Rastignac to lend me his glasses. Madame de Rochegude, bony, haggard, and withered, had sought to repair the premature ravages of passion by means of the devices of the toilet-monger. Just as on that memorable evening at the Variétés when Calyste, now married to Mademoiselle de Grand-lieu, had again encountered her, her fair hair hung down her face in floods which mirrored and threw back the glare of the footlights. Her forehead had some lustre yet; her rouge imposed upon you in the dead white of her complicated complexion. A silk scarf disguised the length of her neck. Her figure was marvellously composed, care being taken to conceal those thin and sinewy arms beneath the ruffles of the sleeves. Madame de Rochegude still possessed that iridescence of silks and moving lights, of muslin and rippling hair, of vivacity, animation and calm, for which there is no single word. I took a good look, too, at Conti. He seemed ill-tempered, absent, bored, and wore the air of one weighing the truth of that aphorism dark and profound: Passion for a woman once abandoned is like a cigar which has gone out— neither must be re-kindled."

One more quotation. It is Rastignac who speaks:

" ' I should have liked to show you Palma, Werbrust, Gobseck, and Gigonnet, that quartet of usurers, cut-throats, and assassins; unfortunately it isn't possible. Gosbeck alone is here, hidden away somewhere in the pit.'

" ' And the others ? '

" ' The scoundrels are so mean that they must club together to buy a ticket costing two francs. They were to hand over their pass-outs so that each of them would see a fourth of the play; but if I am not very much mistaken, that old rascal Gobseck will cheat his partners and stick to his seat till the fall of the curtain.'

" M. de Rastignac made a sign of affection to one of the players in the orchestra, an old man with white hair tuning his double-bass.

" ' Can that be Cousin Pons ? ' I asked.

" ' You forget two things: first, that Pons is dead, and second, that if it were he, he would be wearing a green velvet spencer, both facts being established beyond contradiction in the second part of the *Parents Pauvres*. But if Orestes is no more Pylades still lives, Damon has survived

134

Pythias. It is Schmucke whom you see. The old
boy still lives on the fringe of destitution, without
resources beyond his fifty francs a month from the
theatre and a few lessons on the piano at seventy-
five centimes. He wears his rags so proudly that
it is difficult to help him.'

" ' Could you not point me out Maxime de
Trailles ? '

" ' De Trailles no longer lives in Paris. When
the devil puts on flesh he turns hermit. Maxime,
the brigand, has retired. He is now a married
man and *père de famille*, who delivers speeches at
country shows and takes an interest in cattle and
poultry. *Late* Maxime de Trailles, as it pleases
him to sign his very rare letters.' "

And suddenly the dream is over. The three
thuds of the *régisseur* resound, and the writer
awakes to the contemporary audience—" des têtes
insignifiantes, des galbes communs, des types
ingrats."

I do not know which most to admire—the
repetition of Madame Vauquer's maiden name, in
which particularity the giant's zest is rediscovered:
the faithful adherence to Charles-Edouard de la
Palférine's liaison with Tullia, who for sake of
her lover's dignity sought and procured for her
husband the title of Count: the fine description
of Béatrix, in which Second wilfully repeats Balzac's
own confounding of Rochegude with Rochefide
—one of his rare mistakes: Maxime de Trailles's
last and best *mot*. I have forborne to reproduce
a great deal more concerning du Tillet, who fled

the country after a final bankruptcy brought about by Jenny Cadine and Suzanne du Val-Noble: the children of Madame de Mortsauf, one of whom is dead of consumption, the other an old maid with a passion, *whatever Balzac may have said*, for Félix de Vandenesse: the poet Canalis: Madame Nourrisson, that old hag, now wife of the illustrious Gaudissart: Wenceslas Steinbock, the one and only nuisance in the Comédie Humaine: young Hulot who, neglecting his wife (*née* Crevel) for a dancer at the Opera, makes good his descent.

I owe my first love of Balzac to the opening essay in Mr. George Moore's *Impressions and Opinions*, first read by me on a Christmas Eve of long ago. I have related elsewhere (See *At Half-Past Eight*) how my father was very greatly interested in the stage. He may very well have bought Mr. Moore's little red-backed volume for the sake of the essay about Clairon. Not that my father approved of this writer. *Evelyn Innes* called forth his strictest animadversions, and the *Memoirs of my Dead Life* the liveliest of his contempt. Yet it is to my father's countenancing of this particular volume of Mr. Moore that I owe my knowledge and love of Balzac. Must I be set on a desert island with one author alone, it is Balzac whom I should choose. Dickens takes you up in a great hurly-burly of laughter, and sets you down to something too cloying to be life. Thackeray's mind was, in the last resort, mean. Goethe? I once read Carlyle's translation of *Wilhelm Meister*, and with the last

word of the last interminable page closed for ever
the most colossal bore whom even Germania has
foisted upon a credulous world. Lamb? A
darling, but a trifler. No! Balzac is without
peer.

A younger brother and I took up together the
study of the great man. We saved our pocket-
money and bought the whole series from Mudie's
Library, fifty-two volumes of the Calmann Lévy
Edition, green paper-backs, at a cost, I think, of
tenpence each. How eagerly we ticked them off
as we read! How full were those three years of
their reading! The French gave us a little difficulty,
but we had been well " grounded," and were never
seriously hung up. What a nuisance we were at
the dinner-table, palming off as our own Bixiou's
witticisms or de Marsay's retorts. Once, even,
my brother so far forgot himself as to lean across
the table and, echoing the vacuity of old Poiret,
thus quiz a bearded, Scotch divine who had been
talking bearded, Scotch metaphysics: " Ecoutez,
Monsieur l'Abbé, je voudrais une fois, une seule
fois, avoir le plaisir de vous comprendre." Wherefor
he was dismissed to bed.

I do not suppose that I shall ever read Balzac
again straight through from cover to cover. *Les
Chouans, Louis Lambert, Le Lys dans la Vallée,
Les Paysans, La Recherche de l'Absolu*, and *Séraphita*
are my index of the unreadable. There are deserts
even in such masterpieces as *Illusions Perdues* and
Modeste Mignon. Really I want to read no word
more of the Séchard family and their unending

137

paper-making, of Simon-Babylas Latournelle, clerk to the magistrates at Havre, of Exupère, his offspring, of Butscha, the humpbacked son of a Swedish sailor and a Miss Jacmin of Honfleur. It is, they say, a bad habit to mark and annotate one's books. It is one which I acquired in reading Balzac, and for which I have ever since been profoundly grateful. It enables me now to dip and find the best at once. To underline in youth is to save time in later life.

As I turn over these old volumes I renew my youth. Should I, to-day, think it worth while to preface *Les Employés* with a list of " Personages in the Bureau of M. la Billardière "—a list which you will not find in Cerfberr and Christophe, nor anywhere else, I dare swear, except on that old flyleaf, in the careful handwriting of years ago? Should I to-day take the trouble to record on the title-page of *Béatrix* that Balzac drew Camille Maupin from Georges Sand and Béatrix from Madame d'Agoult. Or that the " Sarah " to whom the book is dedicated is really La Comtesse Emile Guidoboni-Visconti? Where, I wonder, did I discover that precious information? Probably in the letters to Madame Hanska. Would my brother think it worth while to-day solemnly to record on the last page of *La Recherche de l'Absolu*, " Second half much the finer. Balzac evidently not interested in theme? " Would either of us scribble in a margin: " Andoche Finot: editor of the paper for which Etienne Lousteau writes? " Would either of us waste time in drawing up a

genealogical tree of the negligible family of Giguet ?
Let me reproduce it.

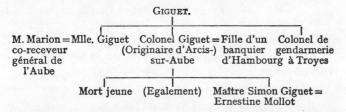

I repeat, all my youth is here. To think of the
hours we spent—this was before we knew of the
" Répertoire " where, unknown, all the work was
done for us—in unravelling these profound relationships. I remember how miserable we were to
leave that poor colonel of gendarmerie at Troyes
in the air, without a name. What happy, happy hours
we spent in fruitless search! I see with infinite
gratification that Cerfberr and Christophe leave
him nameless, too. Perhaps Balzac did not know,
though it is unlike that master of detail not to
have taken the trouble to find out. See how easily
one slips into taking the personages of the
Comédie for flesh and blood !

On another page I find, not a tree, but a branch:

Grévin (notaire) = Mlle. Varlet

Séverine = Philéas Beauvisage

Cécile B.

And yet, to-day, I remember even less of these
people than I do of the kings of England. On
the next page I find an illuminating note:

Fantasies and Impromptus

Beauvisage   = son-in-law to Grévin
Varlet fils   = brother-in-law to Grévin
François Keller = son-in-law to Gondreville
Charles Keller = grandson to Gondreville and nephew
                          to the Maréchale de Castigliano.

Well, these things may be so, or at least I know of no reader in England, except Mr. Gosse, who can gainsay them.

I do not intend that this shall be an essay on Balzac, am resolved that it shall be no more than a sign of brotherhood offered to the true Balzacolater, if any such remain. "Etes-vous balzacien déterminé?" asked Théophile Gautier on the appearance of *La Peau de Chagrin*. Is there a Balzacian left in England? Breathes there yet one who would not find out of place Balzac's reply to Jules Sandeau prattling of an ailing sister: "Let us go back to reality. Who do you think is going to marry Eugénie Grandet?" I used to find sublime and incredible, and now find sublime alone, Balzac's deathbed "Bianchon would have saved me!" "Give me three days to finish my creation!" he implored his doctor. "*Le bon Dieu* took seven!" These, to an older generation, are familiar echoes, but I am persuaded that the new one knows nothing of them or of their great original.

I sometimes wonder whether an abridger, who should have the courage to cut right and left, would not do both mankind and Balzac an immense service. His *longueurs*, his social theories, his reconstituted state render the philosopher in him unreadable to-day. Philosophy has as little to do with the imperishable renown of this grand storyteller and incomparable depictor of character as the dramatic idea, stripped of its clothing of music, has to do with the fame of Richard Wagner. Who cares twopence for the comparison which the Frenchman established between Cuvier, the zoologist, and himself, the reconstructer of the human animal? It was witty of Balzac to point out that when Buffon had painted the lion, an additional stroke served for the lioness whereas the wife of the banker is not necessarily the female of that species. But it was not more than witty. (He returned later to another form of the same idea: " God created the female, man the feminine.") Balzac determined to do for the France of the nineteenth century what the novelists and feuilletonists of their epochs had neglected to do for Rome, Athens, Tyre, Memphis, India and Persia. But those who write for all time do not necessarily write for the day after to-morrow, and although the twenty-ninth century may look back with interest upon the nineteenth, the twentieth has nearer pre-occupations. Those things which Balzac held to be at the root of the social order of his day are to us merely quaint and demoded, without having yet attained the dignity of antiquarian interest. " Christianity and, above all, catholicism, being, as I said in *Le Médecin de Campagne*, an integral system repressive of man's tendency towards depravity, constitute the principal element of the social order." That is not true

now, when the considerations governing mankind
have become purely economic and selfish. (The
Archbishop of Canterbury is not possessed of one-
hundredth part of the power over the minds of his
countrymen which the late Lord Northcliffe or
even the discredited Bottomley possessed; Dean
Inge is less a factor in the lives of Englishmen
than Donoghue.) Balzac eschewed the religious
and political discussions of the moment to write
by the light of " two eternal verities "—religion,
by which he meant no more than the Roman
Catholic form of the Christian faith, and the
monarchy. But have we not seen the descent of
at least one of these from the eternal verity to the
convenience ?

To suppress Balzac as theorist, and to present
him again as storyteller would be, I am persuaded,
to rescue from oblivion the writer who may most
justly be placed next to Shakespeare. Half a loaf
of Balzac would be better than none at all. As a
realist, as an arraigner of folly and all forms of
human imbecility, the Frenchman is without rival.
As a chronicler of virtue he is as insipid as Thackeray,
and almost as mawkish as Dickens. Balzac points
to Ursule Mirouet, Constance Birotteau, Eugénie
Grandet, Marguerite Claes, Eve Chardon, le curé
Bonnet, David Séchard, l'abbé Chaperon, le juge
Popinot, and asks whether these do not solve the
" difficult literary problem of making virtue
interesting." The answer is in the negative. And
Balzac, in his heart of hearts, knew this. I forget
which of his heroines it is to the catalogue of whose

virtues he devotes a whole page, and remember only that the next begins " Cette sotte fille. . . ." Were I the editor of a New Edition of Balzac, I should reduce the virtuous characters to a minimum, just as I would delete Amelia and expunge Tom Pinch. Those whom I would reproduce textually, as they stand, are the buffoons—Phellion that solemn bourgeois, Poiret the ineffable civil servant, M. de Bargeton, for whom I can find no qualification.

There is a quality of biting wit in Balzac, losing which the world is infinitely poorer. " What has a sculptor to gain," asks Joseph Bridau, " by frequenting drawing-rooms wherein men and women have conceived the idea of appearing clothed ? "

Then take that picture of the Bargeton who defies my label.

" Content or otherwise, he smiled. He smiled equally at news of disaster as of good fortune. By slightly varying the shade of his grimace he forced it to answer whatever calls were made upon his intelligence. If he must give token of direct approval he expanded the smile into a laugh, reserving words for the last extremities of intercourse. The *tête-à-tête* was the one embarrassing thing which complicated his vegetable existence, for then he must ransack his empty brain for direct means of expression. Most often he solved the difficulty after the manner of a child: he thought aloud, initiating his interlocutor into the small mysteries of his existence, expressing those minute needs and sensations which, with him, passed for ideas. Avoiding the more imbecile commonplaces he did not talk about the weather, but discussed the things which, to him, were of more intimate importance.

" ' To please Madame de Bargeton I partook this morning of a dish of veal, which she likes very much, but which always gives me indigestion. I know this, yet I cannot resist. Explain that to me if you can! ' "

Hear him at his wife's reception. Rubempré remarks that he is the first to arrive.

" That is natural," replies Bargeton, and Lucien takes the epigram for the sly dig of a jealous husband.

" You live at Noumeau," the good man goes on, " and those who live the farthest away always arrive before those who live the nearest."

" And why is that ? " Lucien asks agreeably.

" *I don't know !* " replies the other, with an air of finality.

" You have not tried to find out," returns Lucien. " A man capable of so profound an observation should be able to fathom the cause."

" Ah! " said M. de Bargeton, " the cause! Eh! Eh! . . ."

Silence fell.

I should like to quote in full the description of all the personages at Madame de Bargeton's soirée, paling, it seems to me, in point of verisimilitude, all the glories of Dickens. There is M. Astolphe de Saintot " who, ignorant as a carp, had nevertheless contributed the articles *Sugar* and *Brandy* to an Encyclopædia of Agriculture, and this by the use of the scissors and previous works dealing with these commodities. Astolphe would remain shut up in his study for whole mornings together, carving corks with a penknife, and dipping into Cicero for the quotable phrase to be dragged in at some dinner-party, the conversation having been carefully steered to that end. This it was which ' entretenait la ville dans ses flatteuses croyances sur M. de Saintot.' "

Here, too, was M. Adrien de Bartas, the musico, and M. Alexandre de Brebian, the dauber, each giving his arm to the other's wife.

" To listen to scandal this arrangement was symbolical. The two women (Madame Charlotte de Brebian) and Fifine (Madame Joséphine de Bartas) both pre-occupied with their shawls, their pieces of lace, their heterogeneous colour-schemes, were gnawed by the desire to be mistaken for Parisians, and systematically neglected their homes. If the two women, screwed into gowns economically designed, presented an arrangement in colour outrageously bizarre, their husbands surrendered themselves, as became artists, to a *laisser aller de province* remarkable to behold. Their threadbare garments gave them the air of supers in a small theatre pretending to be guests at a wedding."

Or take that description of the Vicomtesse de Kergarouët, who was the perfect type of the provincial. " Tall, withered, faded, she was full of hidden pretensions which showed themselves only when they were wounded ; talkative and possessing herself of ideas by sheer dint of prattle, as who should say a round-the-table fluke at billiards, thereby obtaining the reputation of an intellectual; anxious to put the Parisians in their place by a display of provincial commonsense and an insincere parade of departmental happiness. She would abase herself on purpose to be picked up, and show fury at being left on her knees; angle for compliments and never land them; devise a toilet at once careless and exaggerated; mistake the dignity of others for impertinence, and imagine that by taking no notice of people she could over-awe them; refuse that she might be pressed and appear to yield; occupy herself with that which was no longer of interest, and profess astonishment at not being in the fashion. *Enfin*, she could not let an hour pass without reference to Nantes and the high society of Nantes, which she alternately criticised and condemned."

But I could go on quoting for ever.

One passage in *Le Contrat de Mariage* I find doubly underlined. Paul de Manerville has been holding forth to de Marsay on the subject of marriage.

" ' Moi, j'aime l'échange constant et doux de la vie, je veux cette bonne existence ou vous trouvez toujours une femme près de vous.'

" ' C'est un peu leste, le mariage! ' s'écria de Marsay."

In Search of Prince Charming

In Search of Prince Charming

THE grown-up who, at Christmas and for full fourteen weeks after, hath not pantomime in his soul is a pagan. Ibsen is well, and Shaw is well; but at Yuletide Messrs. Wylie and Tate are better.

Some talk of Dan Leno and some of Herbert Campbell, but for me pantomime has always centred in such artists as Harriet Vernon, Ada Blanche, Marie Loftus and Maggie Duggan. Youngsters sometimes ask with wonder in their voice: "And did you then see Maggie plain?" In the mind's eye I see these " principal boys " as though it were but yesterday that they trod the boards, golden visions with their cockades and their diadems, modish riding-whips and jewelled garters. I loved them all, without distinction or faithfulness; captivated now by a bunch of lace pinned at the throat by a diamond the size of a pheasant's egg, now by an elegant phrase of the hand, now by a particularly handsome turn of the heel. About comedians there could be dispute: *tot homines quot* funny-bones ! All principal boys were adorable in their own right.

And then a change came over them which it is hard to define—a leaning to circumspection is, perhaps, the nearest. At any rate, the boys became less dashing. They lost the art of slapping their thighs, and executed that spanking manœuvre, when indeed they did not omit it altogether, with

149

diffidence. They became introspective, sicklied
o'er with the pale cast of thought; and one I
encountered who was positively morose. I confess
that when, last Christmas, I set out on a round of
the pantomimes it was with the intention of re-
discovering not only my lost youth but a lost
young man, the Prince Charming of long ago.
I began with " Cinderella," at the Hippodrome,
and found Miss Clarice Mayne doing exquisite
and dainty things, but hardly those which I wanted
her to do. She annihilated all that the scene-
painters had made to a pink thought in a pink
shade. In the ballroom scene she struck a magnificent pose, black and silver against a world of
rose. Yet, soliloquising mutely over the slipper,
she reminded me less of Prince Charming than of
Lawrence's painting of Kemble's Hamlet. " Alas,
poor Cinders! " she might have been saying, " get
you to your Ugly Sisters' chambers," and so on.
This is not Miss Mayne's fault, but her librettists'.
Do they not know that in such a costume—black
velvet with a rake to it like a cutter's bowsprit—
Harriet Vernon sang " He's a rider ? "

There were two admirable pieces of pantomime.
To be strictly accurate these were dances, executed
with maximum felicity by Messrs. Nervo and
Knox, the " Broker's Men." In possession of the
Baron's kitchen these lively fellows engaged in a
wrestling match, which they then reproduced
after the fashion of the slow-moving cinematograph.
You would have said that the minds of the dancers
had conquered the matter of their bodies, or that

they had compounded with gravitation for a full
minute in which to execute a fall of sixteen feet.
Their deliberate convolutions gave the impression
of a resistant atmosphere supporting the body as
water supports a fish, and the house watched with
the curious tension which the slowing down of
pictures always evokes. Later, the dancers gave
a happy imitation of the classic performers, of a
Nijinsky, in admirable poise, making the best of an
incredibly clumsy and big-footed partner, a Mordkin
à rebours. Here the law was not defied but fulfilled,
since the dancers made it manifest that they had
attained to the grotesque in motion by an understanding of the poetic. It is a pity that the
occasion was not seized to poke a little legitimate
fun at the music of the modern ballet. Mr. Stanley
Lupino showed an engaging personality, but hardly
that of a great droll. He was at his best in a kind
of pin-pricking, deflatory criticism, a reduction to
the point of view of the fellow in the street. He
would ridicule the precious with a glib " You are
under a misapprillusion! " Or he would take a
good look round the Royal Ball-Room and exclaim,
" So this is the Corner House! " Whereby all
sorts of untoward magnificences, including those
of Messrs. Lyons, became one with Nineveh and
Tyre. Apart from these three performers the
success of this pantomime was impersonal. The
costumes were very splendid. The scenery was
of considerable grandeur and elaboration, and
sometimes touched beauty. There was a pretty
wood which had a carpet of apparently real moss,

and an Enchanted Lake, which the programme certified as containing eighteen tons of real water. Real steam assured us that the nymphs who descended into its depths ran no risk of pneumonia, and a decorative touch was added by the real ducks which, in one corner of the lake, signed the picture in the same way that the terriers sign " George Stubbs " in the Welbeck portrait of the Third Duke of Portland. But I did not find here the principal boy of my heart.

Next I sought out " Robinson Crusoe " at the Lyceum. There was plenty for the children here. There was an ogre of such size that his mustachios were human arms. There were marionettes made of gauze interiorly lit up who, on a darkened stage, gave admirable representations of Pip, Squeak, and Wilfred, and lesser celebrities. There was an old-fashioned Transformation Scene, which included a magnificent ballet called the Wonders of the Deep, and the whole ended with a harlequinade. The book too was in verse, which see-sawed quite properly between the heroic couplet and some such lilt of expedience as:

" I regard that man as a wily opossum,
    And whenever I can, I put it across 'im."

"Don't be so familiarity!" said an exuberant crone, and the audience roared. Well, we have authority that the centuries "kiss and commingle," and it is interesting to recall Mistress Quickly's "Didst thou not desire me to be no

152

In Search of Prince Charming

more so familiarity with such poor people?"
Perhaps only those who remembered Vesta Tilley's
exquisite Crusoe and Bert Gilbert's pathetic Friday
realised that the possibilities were insufficiently
explored at the Lyceum where, indeed, there was
a drollery of things rather than of men. But alas !
no principal boy of my dreams.

Again, it was not Miss Nancy Benyon's fault.
She did all that in Mr. Leedham Bantock's view
became a principal boy. But it is in my mind that
in the scene of the stockade the Robinson of long
ago doffed goat-skin for a moment to tell us how
"All of Us Played the Game." In this same
pantomime the idol sang, "Down at Happy
Hampton" in a fawn Melton overcoat, brown
bowler and whanghee cane, and "By the Sad Sea
Waves" in a dinner-jacket, red silk handkerchief,
and straw hat. *Eheu fugaces!* Does this great little
artist really think that in "Lady de Frece" we
can ever forget Vesta Tilley ?

In my search I turned to ways less elegantly
trodden—to wit, the Elephant and Castle, where,
in "Babes in the Wood," I encountered a capital
smell of oranges, a good old-fashioned advertisement curtain, the information that Septuagesima
Sunday is the second after Ascot, but no Prince.
Robin Hood may, or may not, have reproduced the
atmosphere of Thomas Hardy's green woodlanders,
but was in no wise the he of my quest.

At the Kilburn Empire I found "Dick Whitting-
ton," whose hero was eclipsed by the most human
thing in cats I have ever known. "Dog conscious

of dog, attains to Man," says Mr. Lascelles Abercrombie in some erudite volume. Mr. Hallatt's gentlemanly Tom was very human. There was another admirable feline in " Puss in Boots " at the Brixton Theatre, Wee Wally Walters proving that by taking philosophic thought Boy can attain to Cat. It would seem that such an actor and the chief of the tribe of Felidæ are brothers under their skins. I saw this pantomime in the afternoon, and enjoyed it enormously. The audience was composed almost entirely of children, who took the choruses out of the mouths of the singers and sang them with full-throated glee. It was a little disconcerting to find how apt these mites were at the most sophisticated allusions. Let me instance a song which they took up at the first hearing. You must imagine a good, swinging tune to the words:

> " Are you working ?
>> No. Are you ? (*bis*)
> Oh, oh, everywhere you go,
> When you meet a pal you shout—
>> Are you working ?
>> No. Are you ?
> Three cheers for the red, white, and blue,
> Tell me the old, old story,
>> Are you working ?
>> No. Are you ? "

I thought I detected a shade of double-edged raillery in these babes—a hint that, whilst the work-providers may be wholly lax and iniquitous, brother

154

In Search of Prince Charming

Tom, if not Dick and Harry, is not doing so badly out of his enforced idleness. Hundreds and hundreds of tiny tots took up the choruses as though they would burst their little lungs: they roared when the man with the shiny black bag and the worn top-hat tried to get into the Ogre's Castle on the pretext of mending the telephone, or " on behalf of the Prudential ": and when finally the doorkeepers were seduced from their post by a piece of cheese artfully placed within sniffing distance, the mites—whereby I mean the human ones—set up such a yell as would have done credit to their elders at a Cup final.

At this moment I noticed that the little old lady sitting in the next stall was silently wiping her eyes. She had never had children, she said. This being no time for sentiment, I bade her admire that accuracy of natural observation which enabled the Dame to describe rhubarb as " celery gone blood-shot." At once my little lady cheered up. " He's very right, sir; indeed he is! " There were a number of masks here worn by the minor ogres, some of which had the hideousness of Gustave Doré's untempered imaginings, whilst others were simply like the members of my Bridge Club. And still no Prince.

From Brixton to the Hammersmith "Aladdin," wherein two charming ladies toed it exquisitely to the meditative strains of " Thaïs," where there was precious display to outshine Tutankh-Amen, and a man of good address was described as " an old Borstalian." This was a dainty show, but the name-part, as Ada Reeve knew, is one to play " a-lad-in," and no popinjay. Miss Gwen Lewis proved an admirable romp, but no more.

And then I hied me to Kennington. There, in " Cinderella," I found a wonderful quartette of finished pantomime artists. First, Albert le Fre who made the Dame something between Betsey Trotwood and Mr. Albert Rutherston's view of Mrs. Gladstone. Then Harry Claff as the Baron, in well-trained singing voice, and Jack Barty as Buttons, with a speaking voice like all the fog-horns of the P. and O. On the night of my visit the stage-box was full of Mr. Will Evans. Now to play the fool to that austere mentor would seem to be almost as intimidating an experience as when Duse had to let fly at Salvini, in one box, and Ristori in another. But the trio minded it not.

And there I found him whom I sought—the fair, the not too refrigerative, the inexpressive he of long ago. Here was Ouida Macdermott, born to orris-root and patches, ruffling it with inimitable grace and swagger. She was the fellow who had driven four-in-hand along the midnight front at Brighton and upset the Regent returning from a carouse. She was the chap who, in a former incarnation, had put on the gloves with an earlier Harry Preston. This was the lover who

> " hath Dian's wit,
> And in strong proof of chastity well arm'd,
> From love's weak childish bow doth live unharm'd."

In Search of Prince Charming

She, in short, was Prince Charming. For all that, I fancied I detected a shade of uneasiness in Miss Macdermott's gesture. Might it not be out of date to slap a thigh? No, dear lady and dear boy! Slap on! Slap ever! One heart, at least, beats for you.

Twin Nestors

Twin Nestors

ONCE upon a time one would have needed an exceptional reason for publishing that which one had heard at dinner. I plead as my excuse for the present breach not changing time nor altered manners, but extraordinary interest. It seems fitting that the wise things which Mr. A. B. Walkley was invited to say concerning Mr. William Archer, and the witty ripostes of that monitor for once less than austere, should have a larger public than that of some fifty or sixty dramatic critics who, some little time ago, assembled to do honour to the *doyen* of their profession. I have, moreover, further justification for that which, hastily considered, might be deemed an impropriety. The modest banqueting hall at the Adelphi Hotel being divided into two parts by a screen imperfectly sound-proof, it is possible that some profane diner may have broadcasted a necessarily garbled version of these delicate exchanges. Let me set down with something of accuracy the gist of the give and take.

Mr. Walkley began by harking back to a walking-tour of many years ago, and the knapsack with which his companion had beguiled the way, a shaggy contraption of Norwegian design and ornamented with a fringe—a " quite hideous apparatus." Opened, it revealed a leg of mutton! Mr. Archer denied this, yet forbore to disclose

the exact nature of the contents. Yet they should
have leaped to the eyes. What else could they
have been but the works of Ibsen in the original
tongue ? For the walking tour took place during
the time when he whom we had met to honour
was engaged upon those admirable translations,
lasting monuments to his learning, zeal and, I
had almost said, piety. I can imagine the conflict
which raged in that scholarly bosom the night
before the jaunt. Two, with Mr. Walkley, was
perfect company; might not even the Norwegian
giant prove *de trop* ? Here I doubt not that
Mr. Archer bethought him of Hilda Wangel's
" Pligt ! Pligt ! Pligt ! " and at the uncouth
bidding of Duty added to the spare stockings
the spare masterpieces of that astringent, tonic
mind. (Reminiscence permeating us all, I
would fain have revealed how a very young man,
learning the business of a cotton-manufacturer,
used to snatch odd minutes from his loom to " take
in " yet another masterly page of those translations.)
Mr. Walkley alluded to that famous impartiality
which alike caused the American Government to
choose the critic of the *World* as their elucidator
in some forgotten imbroglio, and permitted that
critic, as playwright, to stage in America a melo-
drama full, or presumably full, of all those *trucs*
which he had spent his life in condemning. He
spoke of Mr. Archer's passionate moderation, of
his deliberate avoidance of over-statement and the
striking phrase, and advised the rising generation
of writers upon the drama to emulate these

162

particularities. All of this spoken matter was couched in the most exquisite vein of the polished writer. One reflected that of Mr. Walkley, as of M. Jourdain, it might equally be said, *il y a plus de quarante ans qu'il dit de la prose.*

I could wish that I possessed some knack of friendly lampoon, of burlesque founded upon admiration. To give a true picture of those twin Atlases, bearing between them the world of wit and wisdom, demands the nice pencil of the caricaturist. How, I wondered, would Max have immortalised that unbending Scot towering, not only head and shoulders, but a good half of the torso over his compeer? Would he remember the usher of Ibsen, and impart that hint of awful dignity, that solemnity as of the *accoucheur*, which befits the herald of a genius? Must not his drawing give the lie to him who defined gravity as a mysterious carriage of the body used to conceal the defects of the mind? His subject, you see, possesses not only abnormal seriousness but a mind unusually profound; it needed its possessor's voluntary confession for us to assign to that mind definite limitations. Tchehov, alas, was declared by the eminent critic to be the butt and sea-mark of his utmost sail. . . .

Like his colleague, Mr. Archer spoke of containment and measure. I know those contrary excesses. I remember reading in the paper one morning how, on the previous evening, an American star had burst upon the London public with a radiance eclipsing Bernhardt. On the Saturday following

Fantasies and Impromptus

I was to make my bow to the readers of the *Saturday Review*, and it was indeed heart-breaking that I should have been forestalled in the most momentous discovery made by a dramatic critic since Hazlitt found himself in the Drury Lane pit on the night of Kean's Shylock. I went to the theatre crying with Troilus, " I am giddy; expectation whirls me round," to behold an artless young lady who had not sufficient voice to make herself heard at the back of the stalls. Overvaluation, when it is flagrant, defeats itself. I think our mentors were more anxious that, whilst acclaiming say Miss Thorndike, we should remember the heights reached by geniuses of the order of Rachel, Duse, Siddons. Well, that was a word of excellent warning. The best answer which young blood can make is that Miss Thorndike is our nearest approach to Rachel and those others. It is better, perhaps, for the critic to lose a trifle of proportion if by so doing he can gain the ear of the theatre-going public. There is so much to-day which is not acting, and so much, be it said, which is not allowed to be criticism, that the writer to whom his editor gives leave to speak his mind must not be too hardly blamed if, on occasion, he fill his cup too full.

Mr. Archer started a formidable hare when he spoke of a sterilising, and even paralysing, school of criticism. By this he declared himself directly to mean the brilliant articles which appeared for so many years over the initials " G.B.S." Mr. Archer was not sure that the criticisms had not

done as much harm as good. Because " G.B.S."
would not have written a play in the manner of
Sir Arthur Pinero, he declared, said this critic,
Sir Arthur's play to be bad. I would not commit
the impertinence of defending Mr. Shaw, who
is quite capable of, and probably enjoys, his own
defence. I would rather ask myself how so
penetrating a mind as Mr. Archer's could commit
so curious a misreading. Mr. Shaw's differences
from and with Sir Arthur were the outcome, not
of opposing manners, but of opposite views of
truth. Where the fashionable playwright saw
truth to life there the, at that period, unfashionable
playwright beheld untruth ; and since untruth
in any of its guises had ever the power to rouse
" G.B.S." to berserk rage, it is not surprising
that Sir Arthur's passage through *Saturday*
waters was often stormy. Mr. Archer had more
valuable matter to offer. He discussed the fetishes
of unabridged Shakespeare and uncut Restoration
comedy, and had the courage, and perhaps the
rashness, to say that while Lamb was a fine critic
of acting he knew nothing whatever about plays.
Lamb " was not a dramatic critic in the modern
sense of the phrase." One has often wondered
how Elia would fare were he to be snatched
from the world of the Fainalls and the Mirabels,
the Dorimants and the Lady Touchwoods to
contemplation of our more " real " Janes and
Paulas. Admirably, is the answer. For Lamb is
a recurring Spirit, born ever and again of Fancy
and Common Sense, whose latest topsy-turvy

incarnation is Max. He, you remember, devoted
more space to the play than to the actor; yet who,
when he came to Max's last word, did not feel
that he had seen the play as it was performed?
So Lamb tells us through the actor all that we
want to know of the play. For the drama is an
acted thing, whose component parts are one and
indivisible; and he is a poor critic of the theatre
who shall attempt to divide them.

It was an evening for the bandying of great
names: Lamb, Hazlitt, Sarcey, Lewes, Knight,
Walkley, Archer, Shaw. And if Max was not
mentioned I think I know why. It is because he
holds the secretest place in the temple of critical
delight. That, at least, would be my reason for
not mouthing him.

One Circus for the Rich . . .

One Circus for the Rich . . .

"Try I will; no harm in trying:
Wonder 'tis how little mirth
Keeps the bones of man from lying
On the bed of earth."
A Shropshire Lad, A E. HOUSMAN.

PROMISE a child that you will take him to see
equestrians and a clown and he will set up, says
Mr. Kenneth Grahame, a rhythmic chant of " I'm-
going-to-the-circus! I'm-going-to-the-circus! " As
I dressed for Mr. Bertram Mills's enterprise at
Olympia my head rang to a similar refrain; only
the words were different. " I'm-not-going-to-the-
theatre! I'm-not-going-to-the-theatre! " was my
burden. After the manner of that small youth
who thought that he might like a copy of *The
Pilgrim's Progress* for a birthday present but knew,
definitely, that he would prefer a squirt, I too
often set out for the play knowing how much more
surely I should enjoy the rough and tumble of the
sawdust. Whereas the play is not always good,
for me that other entertainment cannot be bad.
And the less pretentious it is the better.

The circus at Olympia has every quality save
the one which matters most—atmosphere. This
is not Mr. Mills's fault; or at least it is a fault
inherent in the magnitude of his conception. No
man can hire the biggest hall in London, hold up
the High Street with a criss-cross of Rolls-Royces
and charge fifteen shillings for a stall, and yet hope

to vie, in charm, with a page of *Les Frères Zemganno,* or the village show that springs up in the night. There enchantment takes on the true faery quality. It is a fascination compounded of trodden earth and smoky flares, of the sense of theatricality where no theatre should be, of intimacy with a race of people the farthest from the workaday. There wit is freely bandied between the wag of local reputation and the professed clown; there urchins lacking the wherewithal of legitimate entry make sneaking assault upon the canvas; there authority, in the shape of the circus attendant, displays a heavy and healthily soiled hand. Not all the perfumes of Goty can compete with the bruised odour of earth desecrated, yet glorified; a hundred arc-lamps cannot equal the radiance of that single wick of kerosene; the mind of the gold-braided takers of toll delightfully fails to grasp that admission may be a great adventure. Then what setting is the fashionable turmoil of Olympia compared with the bosom of the hills? Since, however, it is an old mistake to complain of one thing that it is not another, I should do this handsome undertaking wrong were I to blame it for not having the merit of a paltry one. Let me say that it did for one moment attain to this peculiar merit. This was immediately after the performance, when we had emerged from the inner temple into the profanity of the booths. A hoarse voice proclaimed that an artist, whom one had to suppose of lesser virtue than the elect of the ring, would now, free of charge, loop the loop on a bicycle.

If you had a good place close to the barrier you could almost touch him, could with certainty appreciate the texture of his fleshings, note the ripple of the muscles, and revel in his immediate glamour. The apparatus of his performance was snail-shaped; and high up, where the horns are, was a little platform with a wooden bicycle. The acrobat climbed to the horns, mounted the machine, spat on his steady hands and set off, to gather breakneck speed in less than a trice. Interiorly he encircled the snail's house a trap opened, and he was safe. This was for me the one thrill of the evening; for once the atmosphere was entirely right.

Given, however, that a circus at Olympia is by site and conditioning precluded from simplicity, I do not see that there was any other course except to pile up extravagance. A crescendo of effect being envisaged, we might, I think, have been first amazed by the smaller glories of tradition, and so become inured to the increasing marvellous. One missed the paper hoops, the bareback riders, the gallant fellows jumping at a venture. One looked in vain for the pair of cream-coloured steeds tearing round the ring bearing, each on its level quarters, a silk-shod *petit-maître*, the two forming a twin pedestal supporting a *Diane chasseresse*, all smirk and prink and coy retreat. There was none of this simple apprenticeship; instead, we were launched into the sheer incredible, and it was as though some tactless virtuoso were to begin his recital with that set-piece and recognised finale,

Liszt's Rhapsodie Hongroise, No. 12. The Olympia circus aims to startle, and it ends by jading. Arithmetically I did not find it quite sound. The programme implied, for instance, that nothing could be funnier than the nine clowns. Yet one must think Grock funnier. Let it be admitted that each clown is one-ninth as funny as that supreme genius; their sum does not amount to Grock. Nor does the whole lunatic congress incline me to forget Auguste, forever helpful and forever in the way. These reservations apart, the show was admirable. There was an exquisite Italian juggler. Everything that Rastelli did was simple in conception, yet infinitely difficult of execution. He juggled with none save beautiful things—fans, flowers, pieces of virtu, skittles of fair shape and boxes of just proportion. Scornful of rehearsal, he arrived from Italy in time to jump into his silk and give a performance as flawless as Cinquevalli's and more decorative, so that with his physical beauty and youthful grace he gave the impression of an artist in whose mind there was a definite, almost concrete, conception of beauty. Eight Scotch collies whose training, the programme assured us, could only have been accomplished by kindness, performed a drama with every appearance of enjoyment; an English thoroughbred went through the paces of the *haute école* as though he had been foaled to that end; forty riderless horses moved in planetary decorum to the voice and whip of their master. (The restricted sugar supply of recent years has not, it would seem, affected our animal-trainers adversely.) Lockhart's Elephants, whose strength and long memory render any certificate as to gentleness of treatment unnecessary, appeared at their most Delsartian; Abdullah's Arab tumblers justified their swarthy race as no pale-faced Council with a mandate could ever hope to do. And then there were the aerial achievements of the Original Seigrist-Silbrons, " a company of absolutely fearless performers who defy the laws of gravitation." I am inclined to think that they do nothing of the sort and that $v = gt$ is true for them as for us. Their cleverness consisted in the skill with which, obedient to ascertained formula, they yet avoided catastrophe. To sum up, this circus, which was the most elaborate I had ever seen, was a fine example to theatrical producers of the inability of magnificence alone to create illusion. One would have given the whole of this great show for a little tent-pole in a little field! But Olympia is not a little field, and the show shone magnificently, according to its lights. Alas! that, perforce, there should have been so many of them.

If I were asked which of all London's Palaces of Delight held for me the most of glamour, I should unhesitatingly reply "The Agricultural Hall." From that day years ago when I, or rather the sweetest little filly that ever owned to three years, carried off two first prizes at the London Hackney Show, the Hall has been a paradise. But then I have not squandered glamour; my secret has been to visit Islington strictly when enchantment has been scheduled, only I have spelt that word HORSES. I have cold-shouldered the noblest professions, steered clear of draper and confectioner, miner and laundry-man, paid heed neither to Mr. Grit the grocer, nor to Mr. Bung the brewer. In short, I have avoided the Hall whenever its main attractions have had fewer legs than four.

When, therefore, the editor of a great and noble paper besought me to take a pound note from his purse and spend it royally on the best entertainment in London—stipulating only that I should render, if not an accurate, at least a picturesque financial account—I had no hesitation. I hied me to the little underground dingle in Kingsway which I, personally, find so much more romantic than Sulby Glen. After expending 2d. or 3d.—in the excitement of the ride, I forgot to note which —and ninepence admission, I was up the slope and past a brand-new traction-engine on a stand, looking proud as a rocking-horse in all his new-found glory of steel-grey and scarlet, with nineteen whole shillings to expend upon adventure, trumperies and gauds.

First I yielded me to a palmist. "Scoffers particularly invited," said the Sibyl, shaking Titian-red locks covered with sequins. Bang went half-a-crown ! " You are fond," said this soothsayer, who had at least the distinction of being the most fallible I had ever met, " you are fond of machinery! " This to me, who abominate motor-cars, aeroplanes, the whole ironmongerish conglomeration! However, I reflected, people who draw bows at a venture

must sometimes hit the wrong target, and I assured
the prophetess that she was entirely right. "Don't
you go being a naughty scoffer no more, then!"
she rejoined, with an arch shake of the sequins.

Next I encountered a friendly camel posted as
sentinel at the entrance to the menagerie. An
interesting fellow, chewing his potato the exact
number of times laid down by Mr. Gladstone for
human mastication. But I left him and his four-
footed brethren until I had disposed of the bipeds.

Now, when Horace said that the art of life was
to *desipere in loco*, he probably meant that at a
world's fair we must take things at their face
value. That night, at Islington, I believed an
incredible number of unbelievable things, beating
to a frazzle Alice's Red Queen who, before breakfast, achieved no more than two. Before that night
was over I managed at least a hundred. I believed,
for example, that the ethnologists are all wrong,
and that the two magnificent African negroes,
wearing headdresses of cock's feathers, were really
Cherokee braves. I believed every word of the
life-history which Togo, of the tribe of Moki
Trogonyte Indians, sold me for a penny. I
believed that rattlesnakes could bite him
"impunely," that in his country the venom of
poisonous snakes is administered to infants with
their milk, that all the pennies contributed by us
went, untouched by Togo, to the support of Togo's
wife and fourteen children in the heart of Mexico.
I believed in the fat woman and the dwarf, in all
the magnificently variegated and exquisitely

175

caparisoned humanity. I believed that, as I saw them in the show, so they lived outside; and refused only to credit that they must, at closing time, get them into shabby suits and indecent bowler hats, or accept that they, who from noon till close upon midnight had been as gods and eke goddesses, should now become plain men and women, even as you, reader, and I.

Next came the theatre where, sitting upon an upturned gingerbeer box, I, like the mad king of Bavaria, was the sole spectator of a drama. A twentieth-century morality play, this! A young lady of blameless aspect was shown first in a pose reminiscent of Botticelli. "*Primavera della vita!* Oh, youth, oh, spring!" I cried. But the lady impresario who managed the curtain repressed my enthusiasm. Next little missy was shown examining an opium-pipe. Next, in a pose of abandonment, holding aloft an empty bottle of Somebody's Cider. "We are compelled to leave a good deal to the imagination!" said my mentor. "Of course," I murmured. "Health Giving way, the Victim feels Remorse!" heralded a tableau which affected me deeply; but "Whilst there is Shame there is Hope!" seemed to me one of those things which might have been expressed differently. I am happy to say that the play came to an end in gloom deep enough to please Mr John Drinkwater.

Let me not too boastfully recount how, with maximum intrepedity and skill at the darts, rings, quoits and skittles, I became the possessor of a sugar-basin, hot-water jug and "binette"—I have sworn that once in my life I will use that vile word. Or too proudly relate how my steed ran a dead-heat for the Derby with that of the fellow at the next turntable—a "tough" of the most cut-throat description. Or how we ran it off, not only once but twice, the judge being still unable to separate us. "'Ere!" said the suspicious pro-prietor, "Wot's all this? Are you two blokes in colloosion?" And giving us each a prize, he bade us be off. After a drink with the fellow of bloodthirsty mien, who turned out to be a harmless baker's assistant, I returned to the menagerie. The catalogue gave no guarantee of accuracy, "as one or more of the specimens may die." Certainly "Prince," the forest-bred, black-maned African lion—heavenly description!—who lolled in one corner of his cage with his tongue despon-dently out, and was prodded to no protest by my stick, seemed mopish. Perhaps he was only bored. The cage opposite gave the lie to the poet's line about "tame and shabby tigers." "Dolly" was a resplendent creature, and seemed not tamed at all. I wish I had space to take you round all the cages. I would invite you to compare the coyote with your moneylender; the porcupine, who runs at his foe backwards, with your income-tax collector; the chattering monkey with the silent member for your constituency. You must imagine these and a hundred other delights. I shall not have room to say even half what I would about the magnificent circus, complete with piebald horses and performing elephants, ringmaster, clowns, equestrians, and equestriennes, "dental gymnasts," trapeze artists who fell into the net from desperate heights, and so gave you the authentic thrill. For one hour I sat enthralled and recovered my youth. Does earth hold a prouder destiny than that of the circus-groom? I was wont to ask my childish self. Even to-day I must think not.

I left the hall jingling three half-crowns, the handsome remainder of my editor's note. I left wondering many things. Whether Mr. Housman was not right about the littlest amount of mirth sufficing to restore man's soul : whether the sugar-basin, hot-water jug, *and binette*, the trophies of my personal prowess, belonged to me or to the proprietor of my paper : whether I might rightfully expend those three half-crowns upon a supper commensurate with the glories of the evening.

But most I wondered which could be the biggest bird in the world, since the menagerie catalogue had given the emu as the second largest, and the ostrich the third. I asked my tram-conductor, but we were back again at the dingle with no more helpful suggestion than the kangaroo.

Like Father Like Sons

Like Father Like Sons

THAT I have never read a critical book about a great actor inclines me to the belief that the thing is impossible of achievement. Only two classes of persons are competent for the job, the critic and the familiar ; and the writer who would pull it off brilliantly must belong to both categories.

Now since, by definition, your " great " actor is not a counterfeiter pure and simple—Coquelin, Tree, and Hare were of this kind—but an arch-hypnotist compelling all transmogrifications within the scope of a single personality, it follows that your critic has the simplest of tasks. Say that he would delineate old Irving. A score of pages will suffice him for the ineffable moiety, Charles I., Lesurques, the Vicar of Wakefield, Robespierre as putative father; twenty more shall distil the quintessential sinister, Louis XI., Dubosc, the nasty fellow of the tumbrils. This little of bulk achieved, he's for his next subject. The heroic habit of the actor is his concern, and not the private fashion of his beaver, the knack of the billycock. These he leaves to your familiar who, with his abundant stores of padding, is faced with the obverse difficulty, the inhibition against the probe. Faithful are the wounds of a friend; but that friendship may endure they must be infrequent also.

I have often pondered a parallel between actor

and despot, first postulating a reversal of a popular misconception. They are kings, and not courtiers, who must needs bask in the sunshine of perpetual approval; majesty it is, not subservience, which fears the chill of criticism. So your actor, more sensitive than any plant of the hothouse. A word of no more than temperate appreciation and straightway his tender shoots are nipped; heap fires of flattery till the green-room pipes gurgle and throb and he will, like the poet's "gradual rose of the dim universe," steal back to radiant life. Like Dr. Johnson, I rarely go behind scenes, where discomfiture, not disillusion, awaits me. A concatenation of events led recently to an unusual breach of rule. As I stood in the presence, yet a little remote, I had liberty to mark the precedent turn of compliment. I caught but a single, re-iterated word—"Wonderful!" Like an island girt by the sea the great actress stood, the tide of wonder leaping at her throat—" yearning up the cliffs to tell "—or lapping her feet according to her admirers' holding in the article of amazement. Momentarily I expected her nerve to give way, to hear her emit some scream of a maddened beach dragged down by the wave. But she stood it, and heroically turned no hair. Then came my turn.

Here let me say that the phenomenon of an eminent actress acquitting herself eminently well does not take my breath away. I expect her so to do. And therefore I confess that I hesitated. The parrot-cry stuck in my throat ; " wonderful " would not, could not, get itself said. Wanting the glib and oily art, and murmuring something about a nice parcelling of emotion, I came the same tactless cropper as that gumph, Cordelia. My reward was not the immediate blasting of a furious old man, but Sybil's tempered smile wherein I read the *mot* of Jenny Lind under a similar provocation: *Il est donc idiot, celui-là ?*

Never is it to be imagined that tactful Mr. Brereton, whose pleasant book[1] about the younger Irvings I have been reading, faltered so. Hear him relate a like story not, in this connection, without significance:

" I supped with ' H.B.' and his wife many times during the run of *The Princess Clementina*. They were joyous occasions, so gay, so free from care. His work done, he was in the airiest and most captivating of moods on these delightful nights. His eyes sparkled with merriment, as he drank his favourite beverage at supper, a weak decoction of champagne and water. He was more like a happy schoolboy than the man, the real man, he was. I remember on one of these happy nights some question arising about the heroine of Mr. Henry Arthur Jones's play, *Dolly Reforming Herself*. Half fearing that I might say something derogatory about the lady of the comedy, he held up a finger, and, with a warning, merry eye, said: ' Be careful, Dolly is a name that is very precious in this house! ' There was a world of love and tenderness in the

[1] *"H. B." and Laurence Irving.*

183

words. 'Dolly' herself could not repress a tear of gladness."

This for me is convincing. Criticism were, indeed, taboo at a board where everything appertaining to the actor, down to his namesake, is sacrosanct. Our author, we may be sure, never defied that precious interdiction.

Yet Mr. Brereton, like all theatrical biographers, invariably prefers those encomiums which, lacking distinction in their setting out, confer nothing of permanence on their object. " I should not," says Lamb of Munden, the great maker of faces, " be surprised to see him some day put out the head of a river-horse: or come forth a pewit, or lapwing, some feathered metamorphosis." What a picture is there here! Mr. Brereton's ideal critic being " one who writes for his readers and not for himself," we find him raking among the ashes of other men's notices and resuscitating withered dissertations upon the " nervous excitement " in " H.B.'s " scene with the Ghost, his " passionate pity " for Hamlet *père*, his " indignation and inception of a scheme of vengeance," his " contempt for his own infirmity of purpose." No picture here that is not appropriate to a wilderness of Hamlets!

Surely safety and flatness can go no farther than the following excerpt from an account of Irving's Edinburgh Hamlet of 1895:—

" Mr. Irving's view of this character is the one which has been adopted by most scholarly men.

The keynote of the impersonation was struck in the mental excitement and unsettlement of thought which results from the message of the ghostly visitant. The commission he receives to avenge the ' foul and most unnatural ' murder is one which Hamlet feels is too heavy a task for him. The times are out of joint, and it is a ' cursed spite ' that it has fallen upon him to set it right."

Coming to the Adelphi Hamlet of 1905 we get this picture, again the result of Mr. Brereton's burrowings:—

" An affectionate disposition turned awry by tragic events is the keynote of Mr. Irving's impersonation."

Whereby we recognise the same intensity of vision which prompted a critic of our own days to record of Mr. Godfrey Tearle's Othello that " the keynote of this impersonation is *jealousy*."

May I be forgiven for thinking that Mr. W. L. Courtney's " brilliant young man whom one could meet round the corner of the next street " does more to keep green the memory of this Hamlet than a score of criticisms " written to please readers ? "

My acquaintance with H. B. Irving was of the slightest. It began in the classic manner. A provincial performance of *Louis XI.*, a comparison by the critic of the actor's make-up with the mask Balzac has recorded—high-thinking forehead and

185

vulgar jowl bespeaking the man of lineage and the
besotted peasant—a request by the actor for the
title of the book, a presentation-copy of *Maître
Cornélius* in the tenpenny Calmann Lévy edition,
an autographed portrait, and finally a meeting at
luncheon.

We each brought seconds, I another innocent,
Irving a satellite whose function seemed to be
ever and anon to bring back the straying conversation to its proper focus. I am quite sure that
the actor was unconscious of this little attention
on the part of his follower, and that he came back
to talk of himself and his art out of a sense of duty
and politeness. (I have often wondered whether
it was Mr. Brereton who on that day played the
rôle of " Charles, his friend.")

At once I remarked that lovableness upon which
my author so loyally and rightly insists. It seemed
to me doubled with a queer humility, a legacy,
doubtless, from the father's proud trick of abase-
ment before his public. The son's manner seemed
to me curiously compounded of royalty and that
disarming, cringing humility which made his
Crichton so admirable a success. You would
have said that the butler's feudality had become
part of the fabric of the actor's mind. At that
luncheon Irving seemed to me to be very much
the player, preposterously cravatted, wilfully
dishevelled as though he held Mathias's bed-
curtains in either hand. It would be improper
to stress an impression gained on so trivial an
occasion, and perhaps Irving was acting, playing

up to my supposed conception of him. Let me write of him as a mummer pure and simple.

On the stage H. B. Irving was exaggeratedly actorish, with an infatuation for " business " almost grotesque. In the Camberwell Hamlet of 1896 we read that " he had a very interesting way of giving the ' To be or not to be ' soliloquy. He entered from the back of the stage reading a book, which he carried in his hand, and was so wrapped in what he was doing that he walked into the table in the centre of the stage. He then seated himself sideways on the table, swinging his leg, and held his hand out over a brazier which contained a live coal, still absorbed in the book. After warming and withdrawing his hand two or three times, he became more absorbed in the book, and withdrew his hand very hurriedly from the brazier, having been brought to a sense of his surroundings evidently by burning his hand. He then sighed and, resting the book on his knee, began the soliloquy." So does your stage-player read the word " interpret."

In his third and last Hamlet Irving had still not succeeded in getting away from the stage. Probably he did not try. The curtain rose up on the second scene of the play, revealing a flight of steps down which the Court presently descended in column of route, coming to attention at the line:

" Though yet of Hamlet our dear brother's
    death. . . ."

187

And amongst them the audience could detect no Prince. The king had concluded his orders for the day, had detailed Voltimand and Cornelius for duty in Norway and given Laertes leave to speak before the young Hamlet condescended to put in an appearance.

This belatedly accomplished, Irving was received at the top of the stairs with a full salvo of limes. " But now, my cousin Hamlet, and my son,—" began the king. " A little more than kin, and less than kind," muttered the sulky youth into his sleeve. " How is it that the clouds still hang on you ? " pursued Claudius. " Not so, my lord; I am too much in the sun," retorted the timid hero, striving without success to evade the limelight's glare. And then the play began.

This Hamlet was an actor's performance from first to last; it got over the footlights, but did not advance beyond the stage.

" H.B.," one would say, was an actor of all but the highest class. A creature, his intimates tell us, of infinite modesty, yet one whose every gesture implied a conception of the actor as the ultimate object of creation, he evoked the storm without the power to dominate it. His nearest approach to genius lay in the portrayal of the *macabre*. His gentleman-burglar in *The Van Dyck* seemed to me to be not " bright and excruciatingly funny," but remarkably sinister. I do not think Irving had it in him to be uncomplicatedly droll.

In connection with *Letty*, Mr. Brereton gives his readers one of the only two real pieces of criticism in his book. He quotes from a letter written to him by Sir A. W. Pinero.

" H. B. Irving's performance in *Letty* was of the kind that is more satisfying to the author than to the public. Essentially it was beautiful. But he was, in the highest sense, as his father was before him, a ' character ' actor ; in ' straight ' parts, as they are called in the theatre, he was hampered by a personality which always had in it something of the quality of grimness. And so, though his understanding of Nevill Letchmere was perfect, the man became in his hands too determined a libertine."

" Essentially it was beautiful " is a fine gesture —a contemptuous kick at that fawning public which Sir Arthur has always had at his feet.

Laurence Irving possessed a strain of genius. His Justice Shallow, the creation of a magnificent character-actor, and one never brought to London, was the most terrifying picture of grotesque ruin ever set upon the stage. Mind and body made a level race of it to the grave. Here Mr. Brereton lands the second of his critical fish.

" You might really go to the theatre regularly for twenty years without seeing so singular a feat of creative imagination by an actor of a minor or middle-aged part. The figure of greedy, timid, boastful, leering, crackling dotage was so delightfully and minutely worked out, so embroidered upon with curious, picturesque little traits, so elaborated into a kind of brilliant and humorous

189

exposition of the whole psychology of senility, and it was all so supremely veracious and so perfect in its cohesion and unity, that the playgoer who saw it was sent back to read this text of the play with a new wonder at the genius of Shakespeare which, by a few broken scraps of speech, could convey to a player the material for such a picture. But it was also with wonder and joy at the cunning genius with which the young artist had put hint and hint together, inferred a human quality or a deficiency from the rhythm of a sentence or the idle repetition of a word, and pieced out that grotesque and awful image of a weak mind's and soul's decay from the broken fragments of drivelling reminiscence in the text."

This passage does not persuade me that the writer would have done better to forego his own pleasure and " write for his readers." That was never Montague's way.

Typhoon, in which Laurence achieved a *tour de force* of impassivity, never seemed to me quite worth while. His Hamlet it was which, in a queer, distorted way, gave glimpses of an individual promise, never, alas! to be fulfilled. The father had played Hamlet with his temperament, and his temperament alone, in his countenance the light of heaven and hell blazed ever romantically. The mask of the elder son was the face of Mephistopheles with the light gone out. With Laurence brain and temperament fused together. Of all the Hamlets I have seen he alone gave full value to those bravura embroideries on a theme of carrion, to the sinister itch, the instinct for rottenness and death, the sickly balancing of craven scruple and bestial oblivion. " Vital and decadent together," I have described this Hamlet in *Buzz, Buzz!* As this book has long been out of print, and is now only to be met with in the 2d. box of the bookseller in the Charing Cross Road, I may perhaps be allowed to transcribe what I wrote on the evening of Laurence's performance all those years ago.

"Atrocious in pure technics, this Hamlet transcended his brother's accurate carpentry. The actor's voice, alternately piping treble and boat-swain's bass, and both beyond control, blew out the phrases like bellying sails; wrong stresses were thick as leaves in Vallombrosa. No poetry here, no passion, the upbraiding of the Queen mere blackguarding. Yet these twists and tor-turings took on a quality that 'H.B.'s' more sophisticated Hamlet knew not. They showed the boy of genius cuffed and cowed by his schoolfellow, the world; inarticulate for all his prating, coltish, unbroken. His voice had the break of adolescence."

Laurence Irving possessed nothing of the one quality which you would have declared to be essential to great acting—rhythm. Yet I know no street at the corner of which I shall meet a figure at once so excessively romantic, challeng-ing, rare.

"Upon this Picture and on This"

"*Upon this Picture and on This*"

THE reader is asked, in that which follows, to consider two plays produced in London towards the end of last year. The first is a comedy by Mr. Ian Hay, entitled *The Happy Ending*. Of its reception the then dramatic critic of the *Sunday Times* wrote: "Prolonged cheers came from the gallery after every act. Shouts for Mr. Loraine and then for Miss Ethel Irving nearly made holes in the ceiling, and even Mr. Fred Kerr, most sober and well-behaved of the ancients in our midst, could scarcely contain himself at the wonderful reception given to every one on the stage." The theatre, of which the ceiling was so nearly damaged, was the St. James's.

To declare that a play can be affected by the theatre in which it is performed seems, at first sight, as absurd as to affirm that the meaning of a book depends upon its print and binding. Yet I think that a play can be so affected. It is conceivable that I might have thought less unfavourably of Mr. Ian Hay's comedy, *The Happy Ending*, if it had been produced in some garish playhouse without a history. But the St. James's Theatre has more than a history; it possesses, for all sophisticated playgoers, a tradition. That elegant ceiling, studded discreetly as the vault of Heaven, the sombre yet rich decorations, the lavish spacing of the stalls—these material things give the place an air. But that which affects me more is insubstantial: it is the memory of a bygone generation of playgoers which, knowing the best in life and art and letters, was accustomed to behold its own features in the mirror held up with charm and discretion by Wilde, Pinero, and other cultivated playwrights. Mr Hay holds up his glass, too, but how different the world mirror'd, hopelessly vulgar in mind and feeling, possessive of every attribute of lower-class consciousness, except common sense!

On the second night there was not more hand - clapping than courtesy to the actors demanded. How could we, not being boors, approve this sympathetic study of bad manners? How could we look with approval on a consenting picture of a social stratum in which the only rule of conduct is " what the neighbours will say ? " It is obvious that a delightful comedy might be written round people belonging to the leisured classes whose mental outlook is that of the servants'-hall. But it would have to be satirical, whereas Mr. Hay's play is ideal. There is, needless to say, no spoken prologue in which the author, coming before the curtain, proclaims his characters to be models for mankind. Such a prologue is unnecessary. Every work of art, from the simple essay to the complicated piece of writing which is a play, possesses what we may call a total gesture, the sum of a thousand straws blown upon a common wind. There are a thousand little touches in Mr. Hay's comedy which, taken in conjunction, tell

196

us that, in its author's view, these creatures of ungentle behaviour are to be considered gentleminded. When the boy, surprised by his mother in the act of kissing the housemaid, says, " I can't resist any one who's fair and fluffy," you feel not that the author has observed some callow youth who would say this, but that in his opinion it is the explanation which may most fittingly be devised. That Mildred Cradock's husband should call the housemaid " dear " in the presence of his wife, and boast openly to Mildred of the number of his mistresses living within a stone's-throw, is not held, you feel, by the author as any bar to consideration of Cradock as an engaging, gentlemanly scoundrel. " I am absolutely heart-whole. All that I want is love, all that I ask is you," the fellow declares to Mildred five minutes later with entire seriousness. And once more you feel that the author is unconscious that he has drawn a blackguard who is also a cad.

The gist of the play is this. Cradock deserted his wife during a shipwreck and went off in another boat with another woman. Mildred subsequently brought up her two daughters and a son in the belief that their father died a hero's death. As Mr. Hay would put it, she has shoved father down the children's throats morning, noon, and night. After fifteen years Cradock turns up again, proposes to resume life with Mildred and to supplement the pocket-money which she allows him by cheating the neighbours at cards. Mildred will make any sacrifice to save the children from contamination.

She will give Cradock a large sum of money to go away. She will send remittances to Hong-Kong. Cradock insists that she shall live with him. " I will invoke the law! " Mildred cries. " You daren't! " Cradock retorts. " You daren't because of the pretty story you have woven about me! You daren't, because the neighbours would laugh at you! " And Mildred hangs her head and confesses that she dares not face that laughter. She compromises. Cradock is to pretend to be an old friend of her husband and, living in an adjacent summer-house, shall contaminate the children from the bottom of the garden. I should have thought it impossible that ever, in the St. James's Theatre, sympathy could be asked for that which follows. Mildred acquiesces in her husband's rogueries, does not boggle at the duping of her daughter's " young man," and turns only when Cradock proposes to debauch her own son. " Children," she cries, " this man is not your father's friend, he is . . ." At this point the younger daughter returns unexpectedly from school and stifles confession. There being one more in the family to contaminate, contamination is allowed to proceed. For Mr. Hay has foreseen, if Mildred has not, the miracle that lies hidden in the heart of a child. Little Molly in five minutes reforms Cradock who, after dinner the same evening, in diving after a baby which happens to be floating in the river at the bottom of the garden, is drowned. Whereupon the *raisonneur* of the piece lifts his hat and returns thanks to God for the family's happy

198

issue out of their afflictions. But the whole play
is stiff with bathos.

London would be the laughing-stock of theatrical
Paris, Berlin, New York, or any capital in the world,
if it were known that rubbish such as this was
offered for the consideration of cultivated people
at a leading West End theatre. And Mr. Hay will
not let us forget at which theatre we are. " Father
for breakfast, father for dinner, father for tea! "
says one of the children. But did not Paula
Tanqueray, on an evening in May, 1893, in this
very theatre, say this of Ellean? On hearing that
Mildred has lost her husband, somebody says
" How careless! " But was it not Lady Bracknell
who, in February, 1895, at this very theatre,
declared that to lose both one's parents looks like
carelessness? Mr. Hay has taken the least happy
leaf out of the book of one of his theatre's librettists,
the page which contains revealed knowledge of
the workings of the ways of Providence. It was
Sir Arthur Pinero who, you remember, suggested
that the Almighty had condoned an illicit intrigue
for such time as it was kept snug, and upset the
lady's brougham as soon as she took the first step
towards making the union decent. Mr. Hay
allows something of human nescience to Mildred.
" I have prayed God to keep you away, but now
He has sent you back to me, *I'm sure I don't know
what for!* " But the *raisonneur*, when he lifts his
hat at the end, has no reasonable doubts. He
thanks God in manly, straightforward fashion in
that he has seen fit to drown Cradock and so save

Mildred from being laughed at by her neighbours. If the ending were altered, if a truly contrite and penitent Cradock were restored, by artificial respiration, to the forgiving bosoms of wife and children—why, then, I think this play might legitimately be . . . transferred to the screen. Think of those shipwreckings and that career of rascality abroad! The author would seem to have considered the possibility of an alternative ending. With the screen in view, or else because he could devise no other method of clearing the stage for the hat-lifting operations of the elderly *radoteur*, the son commands his young woman to get her within doors and prepare the bed and brandy.

The accompanying words are:

" Oh, he'll be all right. They generally are. Artificial respiration, and all that sort of thing. . .

Mr. Loraine, always so good when he is allowed to be gruff and *intransigeant*, strode about the stage like a policeman, and endowed Cradock with about as much charm as we, not being its architect, would attribute to the Monument. Miss Ethel Irving's performance, too, was singularly unpleasing. Throughout she wore that air for which there is, in English, no adequate expression, the air which the French so justly call "*pincé*." This was, perhaps, not the actress's fault ; she battled valiantly, but could not make Mildred less than smug. You felt that the author had insisted upon his heroine shutting her lips tight to keep the goodness " in," as the cookery books say. Perhaps it were better that I should congratulate the actress on getting so thoroughly into the skin of the part. Mildred, you see, *was* charmless, besides being a fool. Miss Irving gave her an admirable costume for daytime wear—the sort of morning wrapper which " Marmee " in *Little Women and Little Wives* would have chosen, with a tasteful knot of ribbons to delight the children. As for the Riviera-like gown and shawl which Miss Irving wore after dinner—frankly, I do not believe that they were to be found in Mildred's wardrobe. One of the evils of your bad play is that it makes good artists appear bad. You would not have imagined that this was the same actress who made such great display of power in Brieux's *Les Trois Filles de M. Dupont,* and of intelligence in Tchehov's *The Cherry Orchard.* Nor could you have divined the great artist who is Miss Jean Cadell hidden beneath the abysmally stupid character-part to which the actress was condemned. Mr. Fred Kerr wandered through the piece disconsolate—a ghost from a better-bred world.

The second play for which I would beg consideration is called *The Rumour.* This is a drama by Mr. C. K. Munro, and was produced by the Stage Society, after their usual custom, for two performances only—Sunday evening and Monday afternoon. Its reception was both cordial and disgruntled. Most of the critics next morning said that it was not a play.

My neighbour on the right, next to whom, curiously enough, I had sat at Mr. Hay's comedy, and who had seemed on that occasion unable to lap his fill, kept up a continual fire of " Too long! " " Too long! " with the enthusiasm and regularity of minute-guns. My neighbour on the left, whom I judged not to have dined, was apparently entranced but, as is the way of the entranced, forbore to applaud. Perhaps he had not the strength. He was in morning dress and wore a red tie. Well, the play *was* long. It was as long as the longest of Mr. Shaw's with the preface thrown in. There were only the very shortest possible intervals or breathing-spaces, and the actors spoke, not nineteen, but nine and ninety to the dozen, so as to get through the prologue, epilogue, four acts, and fourteen scenes, while it was yet night. They only just succeeded.

Mr. Munro's theme was War, and apparently the author was determined to say everything that could be said on this vast subject. Indeed, I cannot think of anything that he did not say, and my one complaint is that he said everything at least four times over. Since the performance the author has come forth into the full light of the *Morning Post* and declared, with much rotundity and circumlocution, that his ideas demand a new art-form. I will not say that a form which was good enough for Æschylus, Shakespeare, Moliere, Sheridan, Wilde and Ibsen, should be good enough for Mr. Munro. What I will say is that Mr. Munro said nothing in four hours which he could not have said better in three. It was not necessary for him to make his young Civil Servant reiterate the phrase " Dirty Dog! " sixteen separate times. Thrice had sufficed, and we should have known the public school product quite as intimately. Nor need he have insisted upon a complete roll-call of all the conspirators. The whole thing was as though the author was a partner in some duplicating concern. But, having made this complaint, let me declare that every act and every scene, prologue and epilogue, were of the most absorbing interest. It was not a play in the sense in which I imagine Mr. Ian Hay to understand that word. There was no " love-interest." Nobody was drowned, even in the flood of talk. This long-winded thing, which was not a play and took the liberty of concerning itself with war-mongers and the wretches on whose behalf war is made, was a devastating, scarifying summing up, and condemnation of, Capitalistic wickedness and folly. Mr. Munro is obviously a well-educated Socialist. I judge him to be a Socialist, not from the cut of his jib when he appeared at the end of the play to cock a mocking eye at the stalls, but from the evidence of his play alone. I judge him to be an educated Socialist, because, with those brains, he could not fail to give us the opposite view, the evil which must ensue from ill-directed Socialism. But " one thing at a time," I can imagine Mr. Munro saying. " We have got Capitalism and we have got War. Let us see what happens when, under the present régime, the two are in conjunction." Conjuncti-vitis is, I am told, a disease of the eye having to do with inflammation of the conjunctiva. " The

203

word would be better employed," I can also imagine Mr. Munro saying, " if it described the folly of a people which allows itself to be inflamed by the Capitalist for his own interest, and the wickedness of that Capitalist turning a blind eye to every consideration, human and moral, except that interest."

The very learned and distinguished critic of the *Times* said that " There are no fewer than six speeches, dealing conscientiously with the war question, point by point, and with a torrent of platitudinous verbiage, just as though it were real life; and we are as bored as though it were real life." It is conceivable that this learned and distinguished gentleman may be bored by real life speeches " dealing conscientiously with the war question." But is it not conceivable that there are people having lost father, brothers, sons, to whom the war has been more than an interruption of the amenities of life, who regard conscientious discussion of the causes of war as something other than a bore ? " The Theatre," my learned friend would doubtless retort, " is not the place for discussion, however conscientious, of such a subject." To which I reply that if it has not been the place hitherto it shall be the place henceforward. That I am utterly wearied of those well-bred entertainments showing how this little amatory pig went to market, and that other stayed at home. That I am sick to death of pretty, ineffective little actresses fluttering like hens in a farmyard before their manly conquerors. That as long as I live I never

204

want to listen again to one of those strong, talkative heroes with no thoughts at all in his head and only one passion. Plays like Mr. Hay's—and most plays on the London commercial stage are of Mr. Hay's kind, only better regulated—bore me, literally, to distraction. I cannot attend. I am entranced to discover in this sprawling thing which is not a play something for the brain to feed on, enraptured to find an open space which we may turn into a battleground for argument, for an intellectual set-to. Let me give the barest summary:

Przimia, pronounced " Shimia," is a small industrial state whose enterprises have been built up by British capital. Its neighbour, with whom it lives in perfect amity, is Loria, an agricultural state from whom, fifty years ago, at the end of a war, the Przimians took territory in accordance with the terms of peace sanctioned by the Great Powers. It occurs to one of our pettifogging, administrative sprigs that his dignity and standing in Przimia, and incidentally his investments, would be more worthily upheld and safeguarded if the Przimians could be persuaded to arm themselves against the revenge which the Lorians " must be meditating." Or if the British Government could be made to see that the safety of British investments in Przimia must not be at the mercy of Przimian laxity. The young sprig stirs up the Hon. Algernon Moodie, British Attaché at the Przimian Legation, who urges Lennard, a Director of the Imperial Armament Association, to divert some of the Lorian munition-supply to Przimia under plea of that country's peril. Lennard knows that there is no danger of an attack by the Lorians, for the simple reason that they have not increased the orders placed with his or any other firm. But Przimia's credit is good; the country is honey-combed with British capital. " If Przimia doesn't pay, somebody else will." So Lennard accepts a large munition order from the Przimian Chancellor whom Moodie has succeeded in frightening. For Moodie has taken care to arouse the Przimians to a sense of their supposed danger, and to suggest the defensive measures to be taken in the case of attack. These precautions against a purely fictitious danger naturally breed distrust in the Przimian mind, and reopen the wounds of fifty years ago. There is a row in a café in the poorer quarters of Przimiprzāk, pronounced Shimishake, and a Lorian is man-handled. At home in England Jones and Smith, returning from business, discuss under a street lamp the manners of these half-civilised races who cannot live at peace with one another, and the proper size of frame in which to grow cucumbers. A financier rings up his stock-broker with instructions *re* his Przimian holdings. —End of Act 1.

The Lorians living in that part of the country which was ceded to Przimia are now thoroughly alarmed. The defensive measures of which the news has leaked out can only be disguised pre-parations for another attack. " Remember how, fifty years ago, etc., etc." Meetings are held at which the Lorians are patriotically exhorted and harangued. One of the meetings is fired upon, and an English girl, sweetheart to a Lorian, is killed. Smith and Jones, under the street lamp, discuss this, together with something further about cucumbers. The Przimian Chancellor, learning that the scare is purely manufactured, comes to Lennard to demand that his order shall be cancelled. Lennard accedes. Just as he, Lennard, is tearing up the Przimian contract, the news arrives that Loria has declared war. The financier rings up his stockbroker and instructs him to buy up all the Przimian stock he can lay his hands on.—End of Act 2.

Downing Street. A Capitalist deputation waits upon the Prime Minister to persuade him that England must come into the war on behalf of British interests in Przimia. The City speaks, a newspaper owner holds forth on behalf of that public opinion which he has manufactured, the voice of Humanity whines. " Has not a British girl been murdered ? Can British women and children in any part of the globe be considered safe if such dastardly outrages, etc., etc. ? " The interests represented by the deputation will withdraw their support from the Government unless the Government intervenes. The Prime Minister promises consideration. And now a Labour deputation arrives. What concern has this country with foreign quarrels ? Labour will not give its blood to fight Capitalist battles, but will go on strike first. Is it reasonable to send thousands and tens of thousands to their deaths to avenge a single murder ? Is it not true that nothing was heard of the girl's death until, a month after the event, the Capitalists discovered intervention to be in their interest, and so raked it up ? Labour will refuse its support if the Government intervenes. The Prime Minister turns this over in his mind. Fearing the Capitalist vote more than the Labour, he springs upon the deputation a romantic and entirely imaginary account of the murder. The girl was shot by the Lorians for refusing to swear not to give away the Lorian plan of attack, which she had learned from her lover. Besides, *if the Przimian industries are destroyed the Przimian demand for British goods will cease, and there will be unemployment at home!* Let the deputation put that interesting consideration in its peaceful pipe and smoke it! The Prime Minister shakes hands graciously. Jones and Smith, again under the street lamp, discuss intervention. Of course, says Jones, if this were a case of Capitalist intrigue, or even of manufactured newspaper opinion, it would be different. But an innocent young English girl, brutally murdered! Can any English women and children be considered safe if etc., etc. ? A British troopship sails.—End of Act 3.

Przimia has won. (Lennard's firm had stopped munition supplies to the Lorians, whose credit failed them.) A British General is decorated. France and Britain arrange the terms of settlement strictly on a basis of self-determination. The Przimians shall have certain tracts of land containing the mineral deposits essential to the industries supported by French and British Capital. The Lorians, being a mountainous folk, shall have certain hill-regions in exchange. The indemnity and reparation amounts to go to the British industries whose property, etc., etc. The Przimian Chancellor harangues the Przimians from the window. Never before has a war been fought so singly in the cause of Right and Justice! The window closed, he resumes his wrangle with the French and British representatives as to what each country is to get out of it. Smith and Jones discuss Przimia's victory. The British troopship returns. Jones's son has been killed. A clergyman proffers futilities. The financier reckons up his gains. The administrative sprig calculates how much he has profited. Curtain.

Now I would ask the reader who is not amused by administrative lies and folly whether there is not burning matter here. I would ask him who believes that war is the tragic result of a high-minded clash of principles whether he is not glad of so good an opportunity to thrash out the opposite view. And I would ask both whether discussion " dealing conscientiously with the war question " is not better fun *in the theatre* than the stale lecheries of the drawing-room. Though it is little to my purpose here I cannot refrain from saying how magnificently the play was acted. The long speeches were delivered with immense skill and effect: by Mr. Edmund Willard with nobility and passion, by Mr. Fred Lewis with unction, by Mr. Alfred Clark with what the Germans call *humor*, by

Fantasies and Impromptus

Mr. Douglas Jefferies with keen appreciation of the vulgar newspaper mind, by Mr. Frederick Sargent with Ministerial irony and precision, by Mr Claude Rains with *fougue* and virtuosity. I am not sure that Mr. Willard's was not one of the greatest feats of oratory to which I have ever listened. His voice is one of singular nobility. My intense loathing of the Hon. Algernon Moodie was the measure of my admiration of Mr. Edmond Breon. But the point I want to make is that even if the play had been read aloud by amateurs sitting in a circle, it is better worth attention to-day than a thousand comedies declining to happy, indeterminate endings.

Mr. Munro's play would not be looked at by any commercial manager outside Bedlam. Mr. Hay's play was produced in every circumstance and expectation of running until the Earth collides with Mars. What can be done to remedy such a state of affairs ? Nothing.

It is curious that the playwright whose work I have chosen to set in opposition to Mr. Munro's should himself be an authority on war. Mr. Hay first sprang into prominence with *The First Hundred Thousand*. Well, that was a good book, or perhaps we may say that it was a book which did good at the time. It took the point of view that war was a great game and that England must necessarily be the best "side." Colonels-in-Chief, addressing their battalions of regular soldiers, invariably draw a picture of brave fellows feverishly spitting,

210

polishing, and pipe-claying against the day when they shall be called upon to uphold the honour of the regiment. Mr. Hay drew an equally delightful, and equally imaginary, portrait of war as it appears to the occasional soldier. Dirt, disease and death may inconveniently accrue, but you cannot make omelettes, etc., etc. The book came out in serial form in a magazine which is to be found on the library table of every well-appointed country-house and club, and is taken up after dinner whenever conversation on grouse-disease or the condition of the coverts languishes. It put amusingly what the leader-writers for the newspapers said seriously. It was the sort of thing which we all wanted to read, and which it was probably good for us at that time that we should read. Worth nothing as literature, *The First Hundred Thousand* was probably worth that number of men to the army. Mr. Hay presumably made a fortune. *The Happy Ending* is bad enough to bring him another.

I know nothing of Mr. Munro, except *The Rumour*. I have given my reasons for believing him to be a Socialist. I, too, have been a Socialist, but only because there was nothing better. The Capitalist is your quintessential *je-m'en-fichiste*, caring nothing for labour except that which he can wring from its sweat. Your Socialist of the present-day upholds the methods of the red-hot criminal. Lacking, therefore, any company of reasoning and reasonable Socialists, I am fain to return to Despotism, to benevolent autocracy, with myself as Grand Despot or Chief Benevolent Autocrat. And the first thing which I should decree, were I, happily, elected to that honourable office, would be that the successful writer should hand over half his fortune, lands, houses, motor-cars, etc., to the unsuccessful writer. I would charge Mr. Munro to divide Mr. Hay's property into two heaps, and I would allow Mr. Hay to choose. If Mr. Hay decided to retain the Rolls-Royce, then Mr. Munro would have to make shift with the Vauxhall. My second decree would have the effect of compelling Mr. Munro to take his too long play to the barber's and get its beard cut. I should order him to cease playing the Repertory fool, and to remember that a play is not a lecture. I should even insist that he insert a sickly love-scene for the benefit of the late-dining playgoer, of whom the poet says so admirably:

> " His belly whimpers in the dun
>   Processes of digestion. . .
> Down the pink champaign of his chops
>   Glucose appreciation drops. . ."

I should ordain that Mr. Munro repeat aloud, one hundred times a day, the passage in which the learned and distinguished dramatic critic of the *Times* points out that " concentration or singleness of impression is the cardinal virtue in drama."

My third decree would be to compel public attendance once a month at the shortened version of *The Rumour*, on the lines of the Unemployment Insurance Acts, 1920 and 1921. There could even be cards, with ingenious little squares for stamps.

There is one other matter which I should feel quite safe in leaving to Mr. Munro's good taste. He would, I feel sure, need no hint from me as to the becomingness of a dedication. His play should bear, on its fair front page, the name of his patron with, in the good old-fashioned style, a full-figg'd parade of his virtues. What these may be I should not presume to dictate: Mr. Munro, as a member of the Great British Public, must know them only too well. But if, amid so much richness, the dedicator should find embarrassment, if the jewels of Mr. Hay's many-coloured wit should sparkle him out of choice—why, then, I should not deem it an impertinence on my part to recall one worthy to adorn the jealous finger of Congreve, Sheridan, or Wilde. " A picnic means sitting on a wasp's nest eating chicken sandwich with a fountain-pen." Wit of this quality transcends, it seems to me, human invention. It is not, I am persuaded, of the study. It is the good fortune of the social observer who, like the astronomer, should have the luck to glue his eye to the telescope at the very moment chosen by a star to burst into luminous life. Lucky Mr. Hay to have been peeping through the keyhole on this bright occasion, to have had his ears so well sharpened. For wit of such quality as this is, we may presume, an infrequent visitor to low life above stairs.

Looking and Leaping

Looking and Leaping

" The fate of the balloon I do not much lament : to make new balloons, is to repeat the feat again. We now know a method of mounting into the air, and, I think, are not likely to know more. . . The first experiment, however, was bold, and deserved applause and reward. But since it has been performed, and its event is known, I had rather now find a medicine that can ease an asthma."

DR. JOHNSON.

" Men have reason to be well satisfied with what God hath thought fit for them, since he has given them (as St. Peter says) πάντα πρὸς ζωὴν καὶ εὐσέβειαν, whatsoever is necessary for the conveniences of life, and information of virtue ; and has put within the reach of their discovery the comfortable provision for this life, and the way that leads to a better. . . If we will disbelieve everything, because we cannot certainly know all things, we shall do much-what as wisely as he who would not use his legs, but sit still and perish, because he had no wings to fly."

Essay on the Human Understanding, LOCKE.

I WAS afraid, oh, I admit that.

I have always been nervous about heights. Mountains terrify me, as do mast-heads, lighthouses, the upper-floors of big hotels, every form of human eyrie.

I would not inhabit New York, that inferno of the somnambulist, for a Labour Leader's ransom. I cannot even suffer the gallery at the theatre. How fearful and dizzy 'tis to cast one's eyes so low! Methinks the actors seem no bigger than their heads. I always feel that in some fit of auto-hypnotism, some attack of sheer funk if you will,

217

Fantasies and Impromptus

I shall throw first my opera-glasses into the pit and myself after them, in desperate retrieval.

It is a common experience for men to dream that they fall, and wake before they reach the ground. I have two dreams in which I hark back to dreadful recollection. One is of a schoolmate who, on a hot August night, stole from his dormitory to the cool swimming-bath, which for some reason had been emptied, and dived...

The other concerns a climbing accident on the Pillar Rock. I suppose it must now be some thirty years ago; at least it is so far distant that I can write of it without emotion, although there was a time when I could not have done so. Indeed, for a year or two afterwards, not only the scarps and crags of Westmoreland but the rolling uplands of Yorkshire filled me with nervous dread. My friend and I—let me say at once that the accident was strictly none of our business, and that we came into it after it was all over—my friend and I had saved seven pounds each and resolved to expend them on a walking-tour in the Lakes. On a Friday afternoon, preceding a Whitsun Bank-Holiday of the early nineties, two youthful wayfarers " might have been observed " trudging on foot along the path which, skirting the lake of Derwentwater, brings the traveller into Borrowdale. Besides his knapsack, each carried his share of a cumbersome photographic apparatus with three legs. Kodaks, films, auto-developers, and all the newfangled rest of it, had not yet come into being. In those days one did one's own developing, printing, mounting,

and scorned the common chemist. I remember
that about this period one took in a quaint little
weekly in which a Mr. Horsley Hinton was wont
to descant upon the artistic possibilities of cotton-
wool, with the aid of which you could do better
than Rembrandt. I am still proud of my view of
Friar's Crag, or whatever the little peninsula is
called which runs out into Derwentwater at so
convenient an angle that the westering sun, casting
his rays on the boles of the trees, turns them into
pools of liquid gold. This is the view upon which
the London and North-Western Railway princi-
pally relies to attract visitors to Lakeland. My
version of it contains a boat in which my friend
romantically sits, reading a tattered *Pickwick*. We
have not met much during the last thirty years.
Austen has given his life to a highly successful
business, and a not quite so successful performance
of the 'cello part in Brahms's quartets; mine has run
to the stringing of sentences. Austen never leaves
Manchester except under compulsion; I return
there upon the like condition. Betaking myself
thither a short time ago upon some business of
lecturing, whom should I see in the front row but
old Austen! I was well under way before my
eye caught sight of his dear, satirical, mocking
countenance. . .

On my way to the train for London—since no
man would sleep in Manchester for the pleasure
of it—we had time for a word or two. We recalled
Rosthwaite, and how we had spent that broiling
Bank Holiday in the conquest of Great Gable,

Scafell, and Scafell Pike, legging it wearily to Seascale as the sun went down. I have never been so tired in all my life as I was on that evening, recollection of that feat of boyish endurance enabling me to understand something of the courageous equipment of Arctic and Himalayan Explorers. Twenty miles, you say, is not much of a march? Remember Einstein, dear reader, and get it into your noddle that fatigue is relative as much as anything else, and that to a growing boy twenty miles under a hot sun, with three mountains and the legs of a camera thrown in—dear, unselfish Austen, who carried the heavier case!—may prove pretty stiff. Next day we returned to Wastdale, and there, at the famous inn, we supped in company with two young men from London who, on the morrow, were to go out climbing. The talk turned naturally to that sport and its risks. Our friends were modest. They were no experts, they said, all of their experience having been obtained in the Isle of Skye during the previous fortnight. On their way south to rejoin their respective Banks they had decided to bag a few Lakeland trophies. We went to bed at ten o'clock, and were to see no more of them until ten o'clock on the morning of the next day but one. . .

Naturally no inquiries were made until, the following evening, the climbers failed to put in an appearance at dinner. Nine, ten, eleven o'clock, and still no sign of them. The people at the inn did not seem over-anxious, saying that climbers often mistook their way home and even made the descent into Ennerdale instead of Wastdale. They did, however, consult the guide, a Swiss who, on hearing that the young men had talked of the Pillar Rock, looked grave. There were only two of them, he remarked, and they had no more than twenty feet of rope whereas, for this expedition, three climbers and thirty feet of rope are recognised as the proper thing. It was arranged that François should proceed early next morning to the rock and report. After breakfast Austen and I, deciding for an easy day, sauntered a mile or two in the direction of the Pillar Mountain. Suddenly, from the top of a low hill, we saw the guide wave to us and start to run in our direction. We ran to meet him. From a distance of three-quarters of a mile he had seen the bodies of two men, roped together, hanging over the Rock.

We returned to the inn and made up the party for retrieval. Arrived within some three hundred yards of the Rock the guide stopped and bade us go on, cut the rope, lay the first man on the stretcher and bring him to the spot where we then stood, and where he, the guide, would remain. François refused absolutely to approach nearer. He would, he said, do more than his share of the carrying, but not one inch nearer the scene of the accident would he go. He must, he said, climb the Rock for a living; and if the Rock were haunted, as for him it would be if he meddled with its dead, he would be afraid to tackle it in the future and so would lose his employment. Upon this declaration we did as we were bid. At that time I had never seen a dead man—we were not allowed to see our schoolfellow—and to make this discovery under conditions of horror put a very great strain upon my nerves. The journey had to be made twice, and for the last mile we converted the stretcher into a rude sleigh pulled by a horse from a neighbouring farm. Nothing, I think, could have exceeded the impression made upon my young mind by that twilight cortège, the black horse dragging the shrouded figure, and the torches which we presently lighted. For some curious reason there had been few visitors at Wastdale at that particular holiday-season, and Austen and I and the two bank clerks had been the last to remain. It was Austen who telegraphed to the parents and would hear of no softening of the news. Better, he said, the sudden shock than the day-long journey of hoping against hope. It was Austen who met the boys' parents at the station and did what he could in the way of comfort, which was to listen. The poor folk seemed to want to talk, to unburden themselves about Willie and Tom, even to a stranger. So for hours Austen sat, an island of comfort around which the tide of this grief surged and wore itself out, at least for that day.

Since then I have had as little stomach for this sport as I at any time have had head. Yet climbers' books delight me, and the subject finds me full of lore. I believe I could hold my own in a mountaineer's talk by the fire, that is if I were sure of returning to town on the following morning. I am as familiar with some of the most famous climbs in the British Isles as though I had been up them. I know the maximum angle at which snow will lie, the etiquette of the mountain, the danger of grass slopes, the difference between the French and English meanings of the word " Alpinist." I read every book about mountaineering that I can get hold of, and yet tremble at the ascent of Snowdon from Llanberis. The spirit is willing; it is the flesh, or at least the nerve-centre controlling fear, which is cowardly. Descents trouble me not at all. I can face with equanimity the coal-mine, the submarine, the downward escalator at Oxford Circus Tube Station. But I am diffident about the return journey, and would rather travel a stage beyond, say to Piccadilly, where there are friendly lifts. *Facilis descensus Averni* was evidently written by a man with a poor head.

Much of the above ran through my mind as I pondered a newspaper invitation to fly to Paris and record my impressions. " Our usual rates, plus, of course, expenses." The inner " shell," I construed that to mean, as well as the " casket." The ghouls! Man was not made to fly, and if he does, it can only be in the face of Providence.

Einstein or no Einstein, four dimensions or forty, of two things one. Either the Supreme Energy, which we call God, is conscious of Man, or it isn't. Either the Original Force is more complicated than Man, or it isn't. There is a school of thinkers which holds this original Energy to be entirely irresponsible for its actions. It created oxygen and hydrogen, but knew nothing about water; it conceived one idea of carbon and another of nitrogen, and never thought of Man! God, according to these benighted, is not even a Mind less sensitive than Man's; He is not a mentality at all, but an Impulse without a Meaning. By some extraordinary piece of ill-luck, that almost infinitely small part of the Universe known as Man succeeded in becoming more intelligent than the whole—a happening surely as non-Euclidean as any other. Two and two make four, say the Positivists, " of themselves; " the Earth goes round the Sun, and the Sun goes round Something Else, and that Something Else revolves . . . and so on to the brainsickliest degree, *because it is so*. These Tupperish gentlemen envisage with the completest equanimity the most appalling " facts." It does not disturb them that if I place the Sun under the foot of the little god in Piccadilly Circus and the Earth in one of the flower-women's baskets, then the nearest of the fixed stars must be located beyond Aberdeen. It does not irk them to imagine a star whose diameter is equal to one astronomical unit, *i.e.* the distance between the earth and the sun; or another whose temperature is 30,000 degrees centigrade; or one whose light takes eight and a half years to reach us. They boggle at none of these things, accepting without dismay the incidence of their happening " by themselves," like the jug which breaks in the housemaid's hand, with Nobody's by-your-leave —and without Anybody's conscious perception except that of the inhabitants of one of the smaller satellites of one of the smaller stars. I like that remark of the casual visitor to the Positivist congregation composed of Dr. Congreve, George Eliot, and Frederic Harrison, that Positivism appeared to consist of three persons and no God.

If Positivism be true, how miserable a thing is life, how puling our poets!

> " The mourner is the favourite of the moon,
>   And the departing sun his glory owes
> To the eternal thoughts of creatures brief,
> Who think the thing that they shall never see.
> Since we must die, how bright the starry track!
> How wonderful in a bereavèd ear
> The Northern wind. . ."

and so on and so forth sings one. I disagree. Since we must die how pitiful the starry track, how gratesome on the ear the softest zephyr! " Any relationship which involves happiness is bound to involve suffering, as life involves death," writes my friend Gerald Gould. Rubbish! Life has no business to involve death, if by death we mean total cessation or not being. The line in the old hymn, " What most I prize, it ne'er was mine," implies that cruelty which would offer a child a toy and take it away again. The potentate who should say to a beggar, " Behold, thou shalt be king for a day," thrusts upon his beneficiary a boon which is less even than its sting. He must also add, " And at evenfall thy kingly desires shall drop from thee."

But all poets talk an infinity of nonsense on this subject. What is it to Rupert Brooke to be

Fantasies and Impromptus

" a pulse in the eternal mind, no less " if he be not more. Mr. Shaw was babbling the other day something about being a part of the infinite now temporarily inhabiting an earthly body. But what if that part of the infinite be not labelled " G.B.S." in perpetuity, and if some day it shall be mingled indifferently with " C.K.S." ?

Maeterlinck has the notion that future conditions will change man by dimensional addition as much as one who from birth has been deaf, dumb and blind would be changed by the addition of these senses. He then asks whether this newly-sensitised being would care two straws for the insensitive log he has ceased to be, whether he would desire a continuance of the old personality. But that, surely, is not the point. We are to look at the matter, not from that completer side as to the existence of which we have no guarantee, but from this unfulfilled one, about which we know something. Ask M. Maeterlinck's wretched creature whether, given M. Maeterlinck's guarantee, he would consent to die, so that *in his place* there might be born a man perfect in all his senses, of whom he should have no knowledge, and who would not remember him—ask him this, and I doubt whether, out of a spirit of pure altruism, he would say " Yes! " Ask him the same question without affording him even the guarantee of a Belgian playwright, ask him whether he will consent not to be, on the offchance that, elsewhere, some other more perfect creature may be born, and I promise you he will say " No ! "

226

And, of course, M. Maeterlinck in his quality of poet is wrong in his analogy. He likens Man to a creature whom he presupposes to be unhappy. There is a wilful perversity here. A man lacking senses which he has never known may be perfectly happy. I am not unhappy because others are more joyous; poor, because others are richer. I carry my happiness under my own hat, thank God! I conceive trees, stones, and the winds of Heaven to be glad and not jealous of each other's motions. I can conceive the lunatic as being the possessor of the most perfect felicity. But let that pass. Certain it is that Man is not wretched in the sense in which the Belgian philosopher presumes his spar of human wreckage to be wretched. He is, on the contrary, extraordinarily happy. Give him health and youth and his five senses, and he will not ask for six. I am content with such space as I may guess at, and take infinite delight in nutshells. I will make shift to come by that spare shirt and the glass of beer, the ballad and the book, which complete delight. It is when one loses health and the first flush of youth, when the eye begins to make conscious adjustment to small print, and stairs grow steeper, and desire less frequent, that one envisages the Compensation to come. Heaven, I feel sure, was invented by a miserable man, or a compassionate man stirred at the sight of misery. It is difficult to understand anybody being unhappy on this earth who is not bored. To face one's creditors, one's judge, or one's mistress in a temper, is not to be unhappy unless the tradesman

227

prove stupid, the magistrate prosy, or the lady reiterative. Inasmuch as they show imagination, insight, and some genius for nagging, life may still remain exciting and therefore happy. I can conceive no motive for suicide save unbearable physical agony, implacable want, and acute boredom such as that occasioned by the later novels of Mr. Wells. But Claudio puts it better:

> " The weariest and most loathed worldly life
> That age, ache, penury, and imprisonment
> Can lay on nature is a paradise
> To what we fear of death."

Claudio sees more clearly than the Duke, whose " Be absolute for death " is of a speciousness that would not deceive an Old Bailey jury of old women and young. Claudio is wrong in one particular only. No reasoning man fears anything " of death "; it is Death itself which affrights him, and not that which he may suffer at its bony hands. It is the absence of the " fiery flood " and " thick-ribbed ice " which appals the man of feeling, to whom to be " blown with restless violence round about the pendent world " is at least better than nothing. It is the dreams that may *not* come when we have shuffled off this mortal coil which give the sensible pause. " Into the dark to fight a giant," said some poet of courage. But suppose there is no giant ?

Some little time ago I spent an afternoon poring over Montaigne. I opened the book at random, and, as it chanced, at the essay entitled: *That to*

Looking and Leaping

Philosophise, is to learne how to die. What skimble-skamble stuff it all is, beginning with Cicero's platitude that " *to Philosophie is no other thing, than for a man to prepare himselfe to death!* That study and contemplation, by withdrawing the soul and severally employing it from the body, is a kind of apprentisage and resemblance of death." The reader knows the old lay: how the contempt of dying ensures tranquillity to the business of living; how the end of our career being death, it is the necessary object of our aim; how it is a vulgar and stupid remedy to refrain from thinking on it; how so great a fellow as Alexander, dying at the age of thirty-three, it is by extraordinary favour that you, reader, have attained to forty; how an Emperor may die by scratching his head with a comb; how a man should face death with a resolute mind, converse, frequent and acquaint himself with death; how he should design nothing so long beforehand, or with such an intent, as to passionate himself to see the end of it; how death should best be desired to seize upon him " whilest I am setting my cabiges, carelesse of her darte, but more of my imperfect garden."

All this I take to be the vainest counsel of perfection. Montaigne holds life too cheap; you would almost deem him in love with "easeful death." All his anecdotes point to the littleness of life. " Cæsar to a tired and crazed Souldier of his guard, who, in the open street, came to him, to beg leave, he might cause himselfe to be put to death; viewing his dicrepit behavour, answered

229

pleasantly: *Dost thou thinke to be alive then ?* "
Or take his story of the Piccard, " who being
upon the ladder ready to be throwen downe,
there was a wench presented unto him, with this
offer that if hee would marrie her, his life should be
saved, who after he had a while beheld her, and
perceiving that she halted, said hastily: *Away, away,
good hangman, make an end of thy business, she limps.*"
" Death," Montaigne goes on, " is lesse to be
feared than nothing, if there were anything lesse
than nothing. Nor alive, nor dead, it doth concern
you nothing. Alive, because you are: Dead,
because you are no more. Moreover, no man
dies before his houre. The time you leave behinde
was no more yours than that which was before
your birth,—and concerneth you no more." Which
is the toy taken from the child who asked not for it
all over again.

" All the time you live you steale it from death:
it is at her charge," says this melancholy counsellor.
And again: " The deadest deaths are the best."
Yet in the very face of this grim philosophising
we find the old boy declaring his age at thirty-
nine years and fourteen days, and adding: " I want
at least as much more." He repeats with gusto
the story of the man " upon the Gibbet calling for
drinke, and the hangman drinking first, said, hee
would not drinke after him, for feare hee should
take the pox of him." Montaigne desired men
to take life as it were a jolly trick, and to quit it
like one of little value. Plump into the middle of
his stoicism we come upon a curious sentence:

"*Death is the beginning of another life,*" a trail of thought which he at once abandons. Bacon does not give us even this comfort. Death in his Essay, so inferior to the Frenchman's, is the weakest passion known to the mind of man. " Revenge triumphs over death; love slights it; honour aspireth to it; grief flieth to it; fear pre-occupateth it," and so on. It has the sweetness of a canticle, " openeth the gate to good fame, extinguisheth envy," and other intolerable nonsense.

It is curious how little allusion I can find to my own pre-occupation: the horror, the boredom, of not being. Montaigne desired at least another nine and thirty years. I doubt whether nine hundred and thirty years would content me. Even in that time I should not be able to read all the books, hear all the music, exhaust all the possible hands at Bridge, explore all the possible gambits at chess. Put it that I am a glutton. Enough in this matter of living seems to me as bad as a meal; too much the only possible feast. None of the great men whom I have quoted seems to have envisaged my particular horror, which must be the ever-present dread of the materialist. Shakespeare is afraid of what may come after death; I, of nothing that there may be, afraid only lest there be nothing. Whatever the kind and gentle spirits whom I have loved have faced, I, too, can face. I pray only, for them as for myself, that it be not *nothing*. Montaigne hints, except for that stray sentence, and Bacon openly declares, that there is nothing, and that nothingness is a consummation devoutly to be wished. On being told that David Hume expressed himself as no more uneasy to think he should *not be* after this life, than that he *had not been* before he began to exist, Johnson replied: " Sir, if he really thinks so, his perceptions are disturbed; he is mad: if he does not think so, he lies." Miss Seward envisaged my particular nail, but without hitting it on the head. " There is one mode of the fear of death, which is certainly absurd; and that is the dread of annihilation, which is only a pleasing sleep without a dream."

JOHNSON: " It is neither pleasing, nor sleep; it is nothing. Now mere existence is so much better than nothing, that one would rather exist even in pain, than not exist."

BOSWELL: "If annihilation be nothing, then existing in pain is not a comparative state, but is a positive evil, which I cannot think we should choose. I must be allowed to differ here; and it would lessen the hope of a future state founded on the argument, that the Supreme Being, who is good as he is great, will hereafter compensate for our present sufferings in this life. For if existence, such as we have it here, be comparatively a good, we have no reason to complain, though no more of it should be given to us. But if our only state of existence were in this world, then we might with some reason complain that we are so dissatisfied with our enjoyments compared with our desires."

JOHNSON: " The lady confounds annihilation, which is nothing, with the apprehension of it, which is dreadful. It is in the apprehension of it that the horror of annihilation consists."

Johnson is wrong. A state of not being, where we might reasonably expect a state of being, is horrible in itself. It is the negation of human purpose whatever it may be of the Divine. Death has stumped our greatest imagists. The rest may be silence, but it is not silence which we should demand from our poets. Balzac's " La gloire est le soleil des morts " is a phrase more shattering than any of Shakespeare, but it remains a phrase. Glory is a poor sun to that which, in the grave, may not even hanker after warmth.

One Englishman alone, and one Frenchman, voice me perfectly. Says Lamb: " Whatsoever thwarts, or puts me out of my way, brings death unto my mind. All partial evils, like humours, run into that capital plague-sore. I have heard some profess an indifference to life. Such hail the end of their existence as a port of refuge; and speak of the grave as of some soft arms, in which they may slumber as on a pillow. Some have wooed death—but out upon thee, I say, thou foul, ugly phantom! I detest, abhor, execrate, and (with Friar John) give thee to six score thousand devils, as in no instance to be excused or tolerated, but shunned as an universal viper; to be branded, proscribed, and spoken evil of! In no way can I be brought to digest thee, thou thin, melancholy *Privation*, or more frightful and confounding *Positive*! Those antidotes, prescribed against the fear of thee, are altogether frigid and insulting, like thyself. For what satisfaction hath a man, that he shall " lie down with kings and emperors in death," who in his lifetime never greatly coveted the society of such bedfellows ? "

But Lamb returns to heartsomeness in the end. " More than all, I conceive disgust at those impertinent and misbecoming familiarities, inscribed upon your ordinary tombstones. Every dead man must take upon himself to be lecturing me with his odious truism, that ' Such as he now is I must shortly be.' Not so shortly, friend, perhaps, as thou imaginest. In the meantime I am alive. I move about. I am worth twenty of thee. Know thy betters! "

Not so the Frenchman. I take those pages in which Maupassant, invoking the dread of Norbert de Varenne, echoes his own, to be among the most disquieting in literature. Norbert and Georges Duroy are walking home from a dinner-party at Madame Walter's. The poet begins on the note: " What matter the little more or the little less of genius, since all must perish ? You," he goes on, " you do not even know what the word means. At your age ' death ' has no significance, at mine it is full of terror. One knows not how, or why, or with what concernancy, but suddenly one *knows*, and everything in life takes on another aspect. For fifteen years I have had consciousness that I carry within me that which, insect-fashion, gnaws my life away. I have *felt* my slow and subtle degradation like that of a decaying mansion. I am so altered that I know myself no more. There

234

is nothing of me left, nothing of the vigour and freshness which was mine at thirty. I have watched death with slow, malignant skill, steal the colour from my hair, take from me my firm skin, muscles, teeth, all that once was my body, and leave me nothing but a soul in despair, which, too, I soon must lose. Yes, Death has crumbled me away, destroyed me by seconds, gently, caressingly. And now all that I do brings him sensibly nearer. . . .

" And never a single being returns, never. . . . We keep the casts of old statues, but my body, face, thoughts, desires, will pass away for ever. And yet there will be born millions, and millions of millions, possessing nose, eyes, forehead, cheeks, and mouth like mine, and I shall not return, nor will anything of me appear in all these creatures, numberless and unlike, for ever unlike, yet resembling each other. Upon what to lean ? To whom cry out our distress ? In what to believe ? All the creeds, with their puerile moralities and egoistical promises, are monstrously stupid. . ."

The matter has been put even better, and with less of hysteria, by Mr. Allan Monkhouse in his early novel, *A Deliverance*, in my opinion one of the most subtle, most moving, and most delicate works in the English language. The temper of this writer, infinitely lofty and serene, empyrean almost, may perhaps unfit him for the lower hurly-burly, but I have never been able to explain his metropolitan neglect except on the score of London's provincialism. We breathe in Monkhouse's pages an air rarer than that of any other living novelist.

Fantasies and Impromptus

Perhaps that is why he routs his critics who, not to beat about the bush, seem to me simply to be put out of countenance by a mind too fine. He is the blind spot of the literary Press—that was only to be expected—but he is also consistently maltreated by fine minds such as Gerald Gould and Rebecca West—Gould, because he never refers to him, Rebecca, because when she does she talks nonsense.

" I feel that Monkhouse is a *train de luxe* waiting at the junction, whereas I am on the platform at the station and cannot get in."

" Waiting, dear lady, for a trip to literary Margate ? " was a rebuke excusable only by my passion for a great, unhampered, chivalrous, neglected author.

I would not insist upon a Heaven for the useful, for those who have fulfilled themselves, who have no further purpose, who are not in any sense creators. That *creation* should be stifled is the dreadful thing; that those who have the power to create beauty should see that power slip from them is that which appals. What assurance have we that there is so much beauty in the universe that it can afford to lose our human sense of it ? Or what guarantee that there is any other thing which we can call the Beautiful outside Man's perception thereof ? It is the *little* artists whose cessation grieves me beyond philosophic comfort. Yorick, Jane Austen, the modish little lady in the pantomime—shall to be nothing be better than to be these ? Shall there not be a future state in

236

which the literary critics shall perceive rarity
when they read?

It was this page of *Bel-Ami* that I fingered
nervously on my way to join the motor-car which
was to take me from the Hôtel Victoria to the
aerodrome. On the way down I saw attached to
the railings of some dingy tabernacle this placard:

> Millions of Chinamen
> have never heard
> of Christ
> Is it nothing to you?

And I wondered what would be my outraged
thoughts if, in Ching-Fu, I should read:

> Millions of Englishmen
> have never heard
> of Confucius
> Is it nothing to you?

Better, it seems to me, to leave Europe and China
to look after themselves. Is it not time that the
Church—and I include all sects, from the Roman
Catholic to the Unitarian—abandoned prose-
lytizing and missionarying, and, leaving the heathen
alone, began again at home on a basis of commonsense? Or even of faith, if you will; but not on
a sly hedging between the two. Is it not time
that our poets began to think less mystically and
less mischievously, that our sentimental essayists
should envisage the possibility of life being a *cul*

de sac ? The passage from the womb to the grave may conceivably be from darkness to darkness, the end of life a bag into which man pitches head-foremost. The real bravery in facing death comes in the realisation that it may really be death, and not an ugly name for something which may turn out to be very pretty. Insufficient credit, surely, is given to the heroism which is without hope. Your martyr, exchanging his copper present for the golden crown of eternity, is pure mercenary. I cannot conceive that the Supreme Being has the mentality assigned to him by bishops and the writers of best-sellers. If He had, He wouldn't be God. Stupid clerics adduce Voltaire's gibbering end as proof of the existence of the Deity. What that end actually proved was the last poltroonery of a great wit.

Consider the soldier who fires point-blank into a wall of dynamite with the moral certainty that here is his end. For him your pulpiteer has never a word. Your churchman cannot conceive that the Agony itself was not agony as human men know it, since it was not mingled with doubt. . .

Is it not time that poets ceased their consolatory tinkle ?

" Thou as a breeze shalt wander thro' the ward,
   Balm to the sick, a cool and vagrant bliss:
   To thee the tired faces shall incline,
   Incline with closing eyes and open mouths.
   Thou, dangerous to men, in prisons shut,
   With life made irretrievable and dark,

Looking and Leaping

Thou on the thirsty place shall drop like dew
Or like a cloud haste to the yearning land.

. . . .

Shalt mellow fruit in the serene noon air,
With rivulets of birds through fields of light,
Causing to fall the indolent misty peach."

Not many weeks before my proposed air-trip I had come across one of those small articles which newspapers more than a century old print under the heading "One Hundred Years Ago." It seemed to me admirably to point Stephen Phillips's views upon the origin of the indolent misty peach. The article related how John Furnell, a private in the 2nd Regiment of Foot, for having stolen the silver spoons belonging to his Officers' Mess was sentenced to receive three hundred lashes. The sentence was carried out on the 23rd of June, 1822. On the 27th the regiment set out to march from Hull to York with the flogged prisoner on the baggage-cart. Furnell died. " On the first day of the inquest one of the jurymen went to see the body, then in a state of putrefaction, and described the bones of the back to be as clear of flesh as if they had been *scraped with a knife!* " Would the poet desire the dead private to take comfort in the thought that the flesh whittled from his body will cause to grow the " indolent misty peach ? "

Is it not time, finally, that we should cease to humbug ourselves with the mere beauty of phrase-making ? For years Stevenson's *Aes Triplex* has

239

been my favourite essay. I have loved that passage which begins: " There is a great deal of very vile nonsense talked upon both sides of the matter: tearing divines reducing life to the dimensions of a mere funeral procession, so short as to be hardly decent; and melancholy unbelievers yearning for the tomb as if it were a world too far away." I have loved, too, that other passage, which may well have been indited with old Montaigne in mind. " Death," says R.L.S., " is to catch people, like an open-pitfall, and in mid-career, laying out vast projects, and planning monstrous foundations, flushed with hope and their mouths full of boastful language. . . ." Then comes the grand passage: " In the hot-fit of life, a tiptoe on the highest point of being, he passes at a bound on to the other side." But how if there be no other side ? " The noise of the mallet and chisel is scarcely quenched, the trumpets are hardly done blowing, when, trailing with him clouds of glory, this happy-starred, full-blooded spirit shoots into the spiritual land." But how if there be no spiritual land ? Once this peroration satisfied me utterly. Now I demand a qualification. I want the meed to be awarded equally to him who, knowing that he goes to nothingness, takes the plunge, and his courage with him.

But since not even a Nelson would cry, " Flight in an ironmonger's contraption or Westminster Abbey!" let me say that I looked and declined to leap. In a word, I did not fly. Peace hath her heroics, but they need not be those of War.

Derby Day

Derby Day

NOT coronation alone exalts our English Kings. One day in each new year their people invest them with new authority, and that day is Derby Day. To bowl along the Epsom Course, smiled upon and smiling, is so much the veritable enthronement, that for England's King to prove unpunctual in this prized respect were to deal at the heart of Monarchy a blow beyond the dreams of Socialism. His Majesty had no horse in the Derby of 1922. Affectionately his people bid him seek this particular victory and ensue it. On this day of days we are all Englishmen together, discarding individual clouts for a livery of common good-fellowship. In those few seconds, threadbare as we reckon time, in which a little bunch of horses climbs the hill, rounds the dread corner and lengthens to a predestined string, the whole Empire is linked in a single interest. How many, to-day, have thought on Calcutta, who else had spared no thought? On the sea a home-coming Prince has listened-in. All over the world the folk who are our kin have echoed the great English poet—" At Epsom—now! "

There was nothing we did not all know about Wednesday's performers. St. Louis in his latest gallops had not pleased. Pondoland had strained his off-hock; he might run, and then again he might not. (This uncertainty had, the previous

Friday, " thrown the market into a chaotic state."
(There is, if you please, a market in these matters!)
In the happier event De Mestre was as confident
of his charge's ability to reverse his recent three-
lengths' defeat at the heels of St. Louis as Descamps
pretends to be of Carpentier's power to avenge
that three-rounds' licking at the fists of Dempsey.
The course would suit Re-echo. Tamar, the
" Manton colt," had been notoriously backward
at Newmarket. Bucks Hussar should be less easy
to beat than on the Knavesmire. Donoghue was
to have the mount on Captain Cuttle. But the
wise man cares not a fig for these things. He
plumps for the name that likes him, scorning the
methods of the stay-at-home who, in office or club,
scribbles on bits of paper and gazes, blear-eyed,
at the tape. Our layman takes his fortune with
an equal grace and, the Downs behind him, forgets
the very names of those on whom, for a furlong's
space, he doted. Where are the horses of yester-
year? The Joker[1]—was he called so?—is dead.
Does " Millais " draw a cab? Perchance, like
" Erin-go-bragh," he earns a king's ransom?
Two noble passions are at work here: the love of
the horse, and the love of gambling. Let none
deny that these are noble. All plastic beauty is
in the horse, the great adventure of life is but a
gamble. Away with the cant that racing has to
do with improving the breed of horses! If it has,
the greater cause for pity. " Le temps ne fait rien

[1] Three popular fancies for the Derby of 1921 were Humorist,
Leighton, and Craig-an-Eran. Humorist won, and was found dead
in his box a few weeks later.

à l'affaire," said Molière in another connection.
The sum of seconds and fractions of seconds in
which a race is run is of the least importance. Had
the horse proved unfeasible, your true sportsman
would have made shift with the tortoise. "Cara-
pace," we should be reading, "has developed a
surprising turn of speed, whilst Crustacea, if not
flurried at the start, is much 'expected' by her
aquarium."

He is neither philosopher nor poet who, on
Derby Day, thinks too deeply on the racing.
Mewed up in that stale prison, the Grand Stand,
the notables see nothing save each other, and that
of which they can read afterwards in the newspapers.
They get the momentary thrill of the finish, but
know nothing of the high meridian joy of spending
a day with the great English past, the price for
which is contact with immediate riff-raff and even
a pocket picked. These be trifles. Of the first
race I, perched in imagination on the dickey of an
old-world drag—actually the hindmost ledge of
a lordly char-à-banc—see nothing. For the second
I stroll to the short-distance starting gate, where
the crowd, thinning ever so slightly, has room to
peel its oranges. "Four for sixpence, better than
wine," urge vendors who have never looked upon
the grape. How good, under the sun, are the
careless gifts of God! One can touch the horses
here and note their pride, and learn that even a
selling-plater has his self-respect. Their riders,
too, are seen to be of authentic littleness. Is it
possible that, in years to come, they will swell to

mean magnificence in snuggery and bar-parlour ? The horses away, we take an idle step in their wake. Little it matters how their fortunes fare, down below, by that self-important, money-grubbing stand; in our sight they have been equal. Next I make my way across the course, put a leg over the barrier, and slip into the common heart. Here a gipsy calls me " pretty fellow "; her man, on his back, unmusically hymns the heavens. Strip them and how little would they resemble the Adam and Eve who, from the walls of Hampton Court, look down upon our time. But on these Downs we are, for a breathing space, free of the trammels of the artist, Mabuse or another, and all the better for that freedom. Here are the coker-nut shies, the candid wastrel, the naïve tipster who, enlightening others, himself cannot put wise. We are close to earth now, to credulity, cheats, the common vision of the late W. P. Frith, Royal Academician, un-recognised Pre-Raphaelite, and Immortal. We are hocussed, surrounded by the language, as Lord Randolph said, not of the Derby but of the Hoax. Idly I note a bookmaker whose board promises prices curiously generous. St. Louis at tens, Tamar at twenties, Psychology at fifties! (In the enclosures you cannot get more than fives, eights, and twenties.) The last of these animals he calls Fizzology, outrivalling in felicity his own ingenious " Lord of Burglary." Suddenly, and with the deftness of a Lupino Lane, he dives with bag and baggage through his screen of tinselled, claret-coloured paper; in ten seconds the defrauded pack is in full cry; later I hear that the police have rescued him and given him sanctuary. Though your bookie be painted one way like a sporting god, the other way he's a shabby fellow. Onward I go. Now stride I knee-deep into flowering broom, that most English of Nature's decorations. At the top of the hill a couple of gipsies' nags, turned loose in the gorse, rehearse for my benefit a scene from Rosa Bonheur. Overhead, ten thousand feet up, some airman blazons with feathery smoke the pale blue vault. He turns and twists, and the drifting advertisement is complete. D..a..i..l..y M... This is, indeed, England. Yet, look you, mock us not . . .

They're off! A brute of little worth leads; the noble fellow who carries my stake is second. " Do bravely, horse! for wot'st thou whom thou movest? " As they disappear round the bend I cut once more across the gorse to see a little flurry of man and beast, no bigger than a pin's head, fly past the post, shrunk to the dimensions of a needle. Across the valley comes a distant cheer. They know the winner in London before I know it here, on the actual Downs. My sluggish fancy, the high-sounding Tamar, lacked guts; he was content with second place. " Captain Cuttle," I take to be, though a victorious, yet a plebeian name! The way home lies between hedges prinked in white lilac, slashed with the golden embroidery of laburnum; the wear of an English bride with the hawthorn in her hair. The children cheer as we were a wedding procession. And so we are,

247

wedded to our love of England. At Tooting Broadway I catch a glimpse of the world's worst statue, and note that to a witless street has been accorded the name of Voltaire. Dear England! I fall into a reverie, and muse upon a better-ordered world, in which Derby Day shall be recognised by those on high, and graced by the bestowal of appropriate Honours. Geniality then shall come by its own. The race-horse owner, trainer, jockey shall be ennobled; even the sporting journalist shall not be overlooked. On my shoulder I feel the not unmerited accolade; in my ear sounds the dream-expected " Rise, Sir——" But it is only the driver announcing, with a tap, that we are back again in Leicester Square.

June, 1922.